MORE TH
REVIEWS A

"If your young child has autism or an autism spectrum disorder the absolute best thing you can do is be treated by Dr. Paparella and her team at UCLA. If you cannot make that happen then you must read every word of this book. More Than Hope will guide you and your child through a very practical and effective journey. You will see dramatic results."

David T. Feinberg, MD, MBA
President University of California Los Angeles Health System
Child and Adolescent Psychiatrist, Los Angeles, USA

"Dr. Tanya Paparella's guidance was absolutely instrumental in helping my child become diagnosis-free. Now Tanya's priceless expertise is available to all families in a content-rich, yet very accessible how-to book. What sets this book apart from the others is its exceptional clarity in communicating powerful information. Using this book, parents see that success is manageable! Now, as a parent-trainer myself, I recommend this book as the essential, indispensable guide for parents seeking help for their young child."

Elizabeth Spalter Iino, MSW, LCSW
Parent and Clinical Social Worker, Vienna, Austria

"Brandon's progress has exceeded even my highest expectations. It feels like, after an almost 3 year infancy Brandon has finally become a real little boy."

Lori E. Holt, Ph.D., ABPP-CN
Parent and Assistant Clinical Professor
Department of Psychiatry, UCLA, USA

"The methods described in this book not only explain how differently our kids process information, but how we can use different methods to reach them. I have used them, and anyone who knew my son a year ago, can see the difference."

Aline N. Osime
Parent, Kigali, Rwanda

"I was lucky enough to have worked with Dr. Tanya Paparella and her colleagues at UCLA who taught me almost everything I know about early intervention in children with ASD. Now parents and caregivers reading this book will have the benefit of Dr. Paparella's knowledge delivered in a clear, comprehensive, and tremendously supportive how to guide that explains what autism is and how parents can provide the essentials of early intervention every day. Of course I wish every parent of a child with ASD could be face to face with Tanya Paparella, but this book provides a terrific alternative. For every parent, the diagnosis of ASD is a journey and I highly recommend this book as your guide."

Sarah Spence, MD, Ph.D.
Pediatric Neurologist, Children's Hospital Boston
Assistant Professor, Harvard Medical School, USA

"An invaluable resource for parents of a suspected or newly diagnosed child on the autism spectrum. It encourages and empowers parents to be proactive and start building a foundation for future learning and social interactions. Wonderfully clear in content and presentation!"

Janis Golob, Psy.D., Certified School Psychologist
New Jersey, USA

"More Than Hope is an invaluable guide for parents, teachers, and paraprofessionals concerned with young children suspect of, or being diagnosed as being on the autism spectrum. Dr. Paparella delineates clearly the major areas of concern for young children on the spectrum and then provides concrete interventions, derived from research and validated clinically over 20 years, reflecting behavioral and developmental approaches. This book will empower parents to assist their child directly and to evaluate alternative services recommended or being provided for their child."

Don McMillan, Ph.D.
Professor Emeritus, Graduate School of Education
University of California Irvine, USA

"More Than Hope is an invaluable resource for parents of children on the autism spectrum. In addition to clear explanations on critical topics, Dr. Paparella provides parents and families with meaningful, easy-to-read strategies and everyday tools to improve their child's development. Dr. Paparella's extensive expertise is valuable to everyone involved in the lives of children on the Autism Spectrum."

Nora D'Angiola, Ph.D., CCC-SLP
Speech and Language Pathologist, Buenos Aires, Argentina

"This book is a masterpiece of efficiency. What a professional book is to the clinician this book will be for parents of a young child with autism. Hundreds of clinical hours condensed into one easy to read book.
Terrific value!"

Stewart B.
Parent, Los Angeles, USA

MORE THAN HOPE

FOR YOUNG CHILDREN ON THE AUTISM SPECTRUM

A Step-By-Step Guide to Everyday Intervention

TANYA PAPARELLA

WITH **LAURENCE LAVELLE**

QUICK LINK LEARNING™

Readers should consult with a professional and follow their recommendations where appropriate. The ideas, strategies, and suggestions contained in this book are not intended as a substitute for consulting with a professional who knows your child and is able to assess whether an intervention is resulting in meaningful changes. The contents of this book should not be relied upon as recommending a specific diagnosis, intervention approach or treatment for any particular child. Information offered in this book is general and is offered with no guarantee on the part of the authors or Quick Link Learning. The authors and publisher disclaim all liability allegedly arising from any information or suggestion in this book. The publisher and authors make no representations or warranties regarding the accuracy and completeness of the contents of this book and specifically disclaim all warranties; including without limitation any implied warranties of fitness for a particular purpose. The names and identifying details of people described in this book have been changed. Any similarity to an actual person is coincidental. Even though an organization, article, website or book is referred to in this work as a citation and/or as a potential source of further information, this does not mean that the author or publisher endorses the information the organization, article, website or book may provide or recommendations it may make. Further, readers should be aware that that web sites and organizations listed in this book may have changed or disappeared between when this book was written and when it is read. No warranty may be created or extended by any promotional statements for this book. Neither the author nor the publisher shall be liable for any damages arising herefrom.

No part of this publication may be reproduced, stored in a retrieval system, or transmitted, in any form or by any means, electronic, mechanical, photocopying, recording, or otherwise, without the prior written permission of the publisher (info@QuickLinkLearning.com).

Published in the United States of America by Quick Link Learning.

First Edition 2012
170 pages

Cover and book design, layout, and photography by Laurence Lavelle.

Copyright © 2012 Tanya Paparella, Laurence Lavelle, Quick Link Learning
All Rights Reserved

QUICK LINK LEARNING™

ISBN-13: 978-0-9851951-0-6

ACKNOWLEDGEMENTS

A heartfelt thanks to the many families and children from whom I have learned so much. Also, throughout my career numerous mentors, colleagues, and clinicians have helped me formulate and develop the ideas expressed in this book, especially Connie Kasari and Stephanny Freeman.

My deep gratitude to those who read earlier versions of this book and generously gave their time and advice to provide me with invaluable feedback and guidance: Bill and Sasha, Steve Forness, Laura Parra, Janis Golob, Elizabeth Iino, Brian Lavelle, Heather Marenda, Renee Marquardt, Sonia, and in particular, David Lavelle.

Finally I would like to thank my husband, Laurence Lavelle, without whose encouragement and partnership this book would not have been written.

ABOUT THE AUTHORS

Dr. Tanya Paparella is a specialist in the field of autism with more than 20 years of intervention and research with children on the autism spectrum. She is currently an Associate Clinical Professor in the Division of Child Psychiatry at the University of California Los Angeles (UCLA), a licensed clinical psychologist, and since 2001 Director of UCLA's Early Childhood Partial Hospitalization Program (ECPHP) which is now an internationally recognized treatment program for young children with autism.

Dr. Paparella holds separate master's degrees in Special Education and Counseling Psychology from Rutgers University, New Jersey, and a BA from the University of Cape Town where she majored in Psychology and French. She also holds a higher education teaching diploma from what is now the University of Johannesburg and prior to coming to the US was tenured faculty at the National School of the Arts, Johannesburg where she taught French. Other spoken languages include Italian and Afrikaans. Dr. Paparella's formative years in autism intervention were at the Douglas Developmental Disabilities Center at Rutgers University from 1990 to 1996, where she designed, implemented, and evaluated educational programs for children on the autism spectrum. Dr. Paparella received her Ph.D. in Educational Psychology from UCLA and completed a two-year National Institute of Mental Health postdoctoral fellowship in the UCLA Division of Child Psychiatry.

Dr. Paparella oversees the daily activities of ECPHP staff and is actively involved in the comprehensive evaluation and treatment of children with autism from 18 months to four years of age. She works closely with parents to support and educate them in all aspects of their child's treatment. Dr. Paparella provides ongoing clinical instruction for students, interns, and M.D. fellows from different specialties. Her clinical and research interests relate to the effectiveness of early intervention – particularly with respect to predictors of outcomes for toddlers on the autism spectrum.

Dr. Laurence Lavelle attended Princeton University and the University of Cape Town graduating with several degrees (Ph.D., M.A., M.Sc.(Dist.), B.Sc.(Hons.), B.Sc.). He has published widely, coauthored many educational books and materials, and received several research and teaching awards including UCLA's highest teaching award – The University Distinguished Teaching Award.

PREFACE

The purpose of this book is to provide parents with immediate intervention strategies that target the core of autism. My intention is not to overload the reader with details, but rather to explain essential intervention strategies that are easy to follow and are known to work.

The strategies throughout this book will give you effective tools to teach your child in everyday activities and tackle autism at its core. Parents can make an enormous difference to their children's development if they know what to do. The earlier the intervention the better and you are at the forefront. However parents of a newly diagnosed child face several emotional and educational challenges. You have to learn about intervention for children on the autism spectrum. It takes time and is complex. Further, identifying and securing appropriate intervention through private, government and/or public means (state, community agencies, school systems) can be daunting. Parents are desperate to intervene immediately yet often face an extended waiting period before formal interventions begin.

I want you to have parent friendly teaching tools that you can use in your everyday activities with your child. My goal is to give you an introductory set of go-to practical strategies that will enable you to begin intervening immediately with long-lasting benefits for your child and your family.

CONTENTS

1 COURAGE

This book is for any parent whose child has just received a diagnosis of autism or suspects that their child may be on the autism spectrum. Whether you need a plan of action or because something about your child does not feel right, you all come to this book with the same starting point. You all have a little one who means the world to you. To even begin questioning that your child may not be developing as he or she should is terrifying. Let alone to tackle autism. So before we begin I recognize how brave you are to have picked up this book. Many people don't realize how much courage it takes to act on that nagging feeling that maybe something isn't right, how scary it is to begin exploring further, how difficult it is to take the next step.

Even though you aren't sitting in front of me, and we aren't face-to face, I am here for you, to support you in your quest for knowledge. My goal is to educate you in a gentle, supportive way. So that regardless of what you take from the content in the book, you feel that I have communicated with you in a manner that any parent would want – with sensitivity, support, empathy and love.

I know because I have sat face-to-face with many parents who are struggling with the thought that their little one is "on the spectrum". Your life has been turned upside down and you don't know what hit you. Beyond just trying to cope with all of your emotions, your family and everyday life, you now have to find out what this all means and what you should do.

Most parents feel completely helpless. This is a whole new unknown and terrifying landscape. Many parents cope with the immediate shock by going into full action mode. They want to know everything there is and want to put a plan of action into place as soon as they can possibly figure out what they need to do. This is where it all becomes even more complicated as there is so much information out there. With the internet now providing a wealth of easily accessible information, you feel lucky that you have so many resources. On the other hand there are many different points of view and competing information. Making decisions as to what to believe and where to start can be overwhelming. I have often thought that autism is one of the most difficult diagnoses for parents. You have so much hope for your child, but trying to sort out where you should start and what you should do is mindboggling. Little is straightforward and the stress on you is enormous. Parents rightly have an intense urgency to do something to heal their child. I have a sense of how desperate you feel and how much you need to be told the truth. After having worked for more than 20 years with parents of children on the autism spectrum, I also know that you need hope and you desperately need to be empowered to help your child. This book will help you with where to begin, and how to begin.

Recent estimates suggest that 1 in every 88 children is diagnosed with autism in the United States[1], making it one of the most prevalent childhood disorders. Tens of millions worldwide are affected by autism. Considerable research is focused on identifying what contributes to autism and the global increase in prevalence. Unfortunately there is no established explanation for this increase to date, although improved diagnostic assessments and increased awareness are two contributing factors. It is generally accepted that autism is most likely a combination of genetics and environmental factors, and it is unlikely that one gene will be linked to autism. Rather there are likely many different genes that could put a child at risk. Similarly, it is possible that unique environmental stressors such as infection and birth trauma may play a different role for each child.

Many parents feel that they are to blame, that they are directly responsible for their child's diagnosis. I cannot emphasize enough – **parents do not cause their child's autism**. We know that ethnicity, geographical location and socioeconomic background do not matter, however we do know that autism is four to five times more likely in boys than in girls. Even though boys are affected at a much higher rate than girls, in this book I reference boys and girls more or less equally. You will see that each chapter uses either a male or a female child when I am explaining concepts and providing examples to illustrate a technique, and the chapters alternate in terms of which sex is referenced.

First I want you to know that **young children on the autism spectrum can make enormous change and achieve what seemed impossible**[2&3]. The effects of early intervention can be astounding. A few weeks after a child starts treatment, often the first observation that parents report is that their child wants to be near them, seeks them out, wants to engage. Sometimes parents report they want to interact with their brother or sister, something they never did before. These are just the beginning steps. Many children can make incredible changes in their development, especially in the areas that are concerning you most. Yes, it is hard work for everyone involved. The changes don't occur overnight, but you will be in awe of your child's development and learning. Each small change is exciting and inspiring and will reward you for all your efforts.

Children all learn differently. There is no one solution. What one child learns first, another will learn later. But they all learn and they all change. Never pre-judge how a child will learn. We especially cannot tell in the little ones. In my clinic when we think back on children before intervention started and how they look even after 3 months, it can be hard to believe. Many parents say to me after 3 months "He is a completely different child. His brain has changed." So we take every new little one that walks in the door and work with them as if the sky is the limit. We owe them that.

My hope is that this book will provide you with the tools to do the same. **Intervention**, **early**, can be **extremely powerful**. My goal is to educate and empower you to immediately intervene and make informed decisions for you and your child. Too often critical opportunities are lost when children have to wait for professional therapy due to huge demand and long waiting lists.

After reading this book you should have a good understanding of the core symptoms of autism and know what to look for when deciding whether to try a new therapy. Most importantly you will know how to implement your own interventions 24/7.

My expertise is beginning intervention with very young children who are recently diagnosed or whose parents suspect that their child may be on the autism spectrum. In my clinic we treat children as young as two years of age who have had little or no previous intervention. **We focus on the areas of development that are considered to be at the core of autism, exactly the areas that are covered in this book. This is a powerful approach, one that has achieved excellent results over many years**[4].

We are going to cover the areas that lie at the center of the disorder. These are the areas where your child needs specific targeted help. Instead of letting autism take hold and progress, I will provide you with **intervention strategies that target autism at the core**. I am not going to focus on any one intervention approach. We are going to focus on the content of what your child needs to learn, and we are going to use different intervention approaches to do that.

We will begin with communication and language. Chapters 3 and 4 explain why children on the autism spectrum have difficulties understanding language and communicating. Included will be **specific strategies** to improve your child's understanding and communication. Then in chapters 5, 6 and 7 we will target social development. We know that there are several areas of social development that can make a significant difference to a child's later success. You will learn to intervene in those early developing social areas that will make a lasting difference to your child's development. The ability to share experiences with others is critical. In chapters 5 and 6, I explain what this is and how you can begin to develop it in your child. The ability to imitate others is essential. In chapter 7, I discuss the importance of imitation and how to teach it. Chapter 8 explains how to change unusual behaviors that interfere with your child's development. If you target the above areas, you will be targeting the center of where autism is taking hold. The sooner you start the better. You cannot start too early, and you can make a significant impact. Chapter 9 discusses different intervention approaches, both educational and biomedical. It is meant to give you some additional direction as you begin to organize further intervention for your child.

The **Table of Contents** in the front of the book is purposefully detailed to provide you with a clear and easy way to immediately access and return to main concepts throughout the book.

Each chapter is carefully organized to facilitate a clear understanding of why the content is important and how to use it to help your child. In each chapter you will find information on what we see in typically developing children and how children on the autism spectrum are different. In most chapters you will find one or more sections called **Strategies for Change**, these are powerful intervention strategies for changing the course of your child's development.

The toys used in the teaching examples are commonplace and at times are purposely simplified (for example, toy photos in chapters 7 and 8) to demonstrate that you can effectively use what you may already have at home.

Each chapter ends with **Key Points** and they are for quick reference any time you need a reminder of the important concepts covered in that chapter. I encourage you to return to sections throughout the book that are of particular significance to your child and reread them several times. Refer to them regularly as you use the intervention strategies.

The blank page at the end of each chapter titled **Personal Notes** is meant for you to use in whatever way suits you best. You might use it to make note of observations regarding your child, perhaps where you want to begin intervening, or to record skills that your child has learned.

This book is a hands-on, practical and easy to read guide on how to immediately implement effective intervention strategies that work. It is not meant to be comprehensive. You will find many books on autism written by parents and professionals. Some provide a general guide on how to access educational services for your child. Others describe intervention approaches in depth for clinicians and professionals. But often it takes a while for parents to figure it all out. In the meantime parents are desperate for guidance on what they can begin to do right away to help their child. Unfortunately just finding and securing good intervention services for your child can take months. This is vital time that you and your child cannot afford to lose.

I recognize that many parents work full time, some work part-time, and regardless of how much time any parent has to spend with a child, most lead very busy lives. In general this book provides you with parent friendly teaching tools that you can use in your everyday activities. Regardless of how busy you may be, every parent will benefit from first reading the book from start to finish before you begin implementing any teaching strategies. Since each chapter may offer insight on your child, you should be able to gain a preliminary understanding of what is involved that will help you decide where you want to begin.

Whether you are working part-time or full-time, chapters 3, 4, 5 and 6 provide strategies that can be incorporated into everyday routine activities. For example they are effective during mealtimes, when your child is in the bath, changing a diaper, before bedtime, or during a walk. Chapter 8 (Change Unusual Behaviors) may appear to require more time and effort on your part. However, if your time is limited, I suggest that you take one or two strategies from the chapter that are not only relevant for your child but that also seem easier for you to implement and begin to apply them during everyday activities. I provide suggestions in the chapter on how you can do this. Any parent with limited time should consider leaving the strategies in chapter 7 (Imitation) until last as they require more focus and time.

No matter your circumstance, take what you can and use it. Any intervention will be better than nothing. The strategies and content in this book are used in professional treatment programs and have been shown to work. They are essential for changing your child's development and **you can begin intervening immediately**[5-7].

PERSONAL NOTES

2 THE CORE OF AUTISM

Before we think about how to intervene, it is important that we first understand the characteristics of autism. Because of the way that it presents in children, autism is considered a **social communication disorder**. Children on the autism spectrum have difficulty engaging in social interactions with other people. They have difficulty communicating nonverbally (through gestures) and verbally (with language) the way that typical children do, and they respond differently to their everyday environment. It isn't easy to describe the difference succinctly, except to say that children on the autism spectrum often focus on unusual aspects of their environment - on things that typical children do not focus on. They may also react to changes in their environment with an inflexibility that is beyond what is considered normal. However this isn't always obvious in young children. A last and essential piece of information to keep in mind, is that these three key characteristics (atypical social development, communication difficulties and unusual responses to the environment) must be evident before the age of 3 for a child to receive a diagnosis of autism.[1] However, while these three areas are identified as the defining characteristics of an autism spectrum diagnosis, autism is not straightforward; there can be **enormous variation in the way that children show symptoms.**

Many parents are confused or discount the possibility of autism spectrum disorder (ASD) because their child doesn't exactly fit the symptoms. Here are some examples of what parents have said to me: "I wondered about it, but my child is very affectionate. Children with autism aren't affectionate. So I thought he couldn't possibly have autism." "I always thought he was too good, too content doing his own thing. But I thought that he was just an independent child. Maybe some children just don't want to play." "I knew she was much more interested in shapes than other children. But I thought it was cute, that she just had a personality with very clear interests." "I began to realize that my child didn't play with other children. But he learned to talk more or less on time. Children with autism don't talk." "My child is smart. She is smarter than other children at her preschool. There is no way she can have autism."

Autism is far from black and white which is why professionals have chosen the term "autism spectrum". This means that the core features will present somewhat differently in every child. Also, a child can present with very mild symptoms or more severe symptoms. A lot of misconceptions still exist, and many people still think about autism too concretely. In this book when I explain something I will usually do so in more general terms, but what is uniquely applicable to every child with autism is that he or she will have some difficulty with communication, the quality of his or her social interaction will feel lacking, and his or her responses to the environment will be unusual.

When we consider very young children in particular, we have to think very broadly. Part of the reason for this is the way that autism often emerges. The onset isn't obvious or sudden. Rather, children seem to show increasing signs of autism gradually. We know that babies at 6 months of age may not show any clear symptoms of autism. Some indications may begin to show at 12 months and increase in the second year, and actual symptoms may continue to emerge gradually in the third year.

EARLY SIGNS

Although autism may not be clearly identifiable in the first two years, there are warning signs. The presence of some of these "red flags" does not mean that an infant has autism. However they do highlight areas of early development that are considered atypical and that may fit with the way autism manifests.

First Year

- Limited eye-contact
- Does not readily reciprocate your smile
- Lack of warm, joyful expressions with directed gaze
- Difficult to engage in baby games like peek-a-boo
- Lack of anticipatory movements in response to interaction
- Does not seem interested in other people
- More interest in objects than people

Second Year

- Does not respond when name is called
- Does not make eye-contact and smile at the same time
- Does not look at objects that another person is looking at
- Does not try to engage people in activities or interests
- Lack of sharing interest or enjoyment
- Lack of pointing and showing to share interest
- Limited use of gestures
- Uses person's hand as tool without eye-contact

Other Warning Signs

- May develop language and/or social skills normally, then lose some or all
- Engages in repetitive body movements (e.g. hand flapping)
- Fixates on objects
- Seems oversensitive to sounds, texture or lights
- Low muscle tone
- May not tolerate change in routine or environment (e.g. a new bottle)
- Difficulty calming when distressed
- Uses objects and/or toys in a nonfunctional manner
- Lacks meaningful play

If you are seeing **several** of these early signs in your child, I strongly suggest that you follow up with a professional evaluation. You can raise your concerns with your pediatrician. He or she should ask you some simple questions using the Modified Checklist for Autism in Toddlers, or M-CHAT[2] (see appendix) or a similar assessment which can screen specifically for autism. If necessary he/she would then refer your child for a more comprehensive developmental evaluation. A developmental pediatrician, psychologist, psychiatrist or a neurologist usually conducts this type of evaluation. You can also contact one of these specialists directly. He/she may administer a variety of assessments which look closely at your child's responding to language and social cues, and learning from the environment. The assessments usually include formal testing to assess a child's cognitive development and diagnosis.

Many parents want to know if there are specific tests that will tell them where the problem is in the brain. There aren't any. Autism, or the characteristics associated with autism, cannot be located in one area of the brain. All of the assessments are based on observation (whether informal or formal) in conjunction with information provided by parents. I am not talking here about medical complications. I am only referring to how we diagnose autism and the social communication components that are characteristic of autism.

It is tempting to discount autism because your child is affectionate, or because he or she is smart. I bring this up because I know how difficult it is to try and come to terms with the idea that your child may not be developing typically, never mind have something as serious as autism. If I was wondering about my child, I would want to throw every possibility out the window as fast as I could. Don't, you owe it to your child, to yourself, and to your family to think more broadly. Be open to the idea that autism presents in many different ways - for some children it really isn't obvious.

To be clear, this book does not set out to answer the question "Does my child have autism?" Just as you would seek professional help for any other medical or psychological diagnosis, you should do the same if you suspect that your child may be on the autism spectrum. This book does however give you a deeper understanding of how autism presents in children and will provide you with tools to boost your child's development.

KEY POINTS

- Children on the autism spectrum have difficulties with communication, social interaction, and how they respond to their everyday environment.

- Autism is a spectrum disorder. This means that the degree to which we see the symptoms can vary widely.

- Sometimes symptoms emerge gradually and may not be clear until the third year.

- Take heed of the "red flags" and follow-up with a professional evaluation.

- To change your child's development focus on areas that most affect children on the autism spectrum (communication, social interaction, flexible responding to their everyday environment).

- By intervening at the "core" you are targeting the heart of the disorder.

PERSONAL NOTES

3 UNDERSTANDING LANGUAGE

Why isn't my child talking like other children his/her age? This is one of the most frequent questions that parents ask. It may be clear to you that your child's language is delayed. The question is why? Is it a problem or not?

Before children can talk they need to understand and learn the language they hear. Parents of children with an autism spectrum diagnosis often report that one of their first concerns was whether their child could hear properly because they did not respond to their name or look up when called. Often the child does not follow simple directions, such as "Come to mommy" or "Get your pajamas." Sometimes, it seems that the child understands some nouns, e.g. "cookie" or "juice" or "train," but not others that you would have expected, e.g. "shoe." While there may be some signs of understanding, they are often inconsistent. In most cases parents take their child for a hearing test and the results indicate their child's hearing is absolutely normal. **For children on the autism spectrum this inconsistent responding, or for some children, very little responding, is often an indicator that they are not learning language from their natural environment** the way that typical children do. They may hear you but do not process what you are saying and as a result they do not understand what you are asking.

TYPICAL LANGUAGE DEVELOPMENT

Children who are developing typically learn language from their everyday natural environment. Between 5 and 10 months they turn their head towards a sound. By 11 to 14 months infants usually turn toward a person calling their name. They also show an understanding of words that are a part of their daily routines (bottle, juice) by vocalizing or looking in the direction of the object to indicate their understanding. At this age half the time they briefly stop an activity or change direction when they hear "no" or "stop." They hold up their arms for "up." By 16 to 22 months children follow simple directions ("Give the car to mommy") and show they can identify objects or pictures by looking or gesturing to them ("Where is the chair?") By 23 to 32 months they recognize some parts of their body (eyes, mouth, tummy) and follow directions with two steps ("Get the diaper and give it to me.") Children begin to understand action words (sleeping, eating) and can demonstrate how objects are used ("Show me how you eat") between approximately 33 and 44 months.

LANGUAGE AND MY CHILD

The following five reasons are likely contributing to why your child does not understand language to the same extent as a typical child. The first three reasons are closely related as they all describe attention differences in children on the autism spectrum.

Exclusive Focus

Some children on the autism spectrum are not attending to the multi-faceted aspects of their everyday environment. They are so focused on their preferred toy or activity that they do not process language occurring around them. For example a typical child looking at her favorite book will look up if the doorbell rings, the door opens and her mom greets a visitor. The child with autism may be so focused on her book that she does not pay attention to any of these events and misses a natural learning opportunity.

Difficulty Shifting Attention

Children on the autism spectrum often have difficulty shifting their attention from one thing to another. For example if a typical child is playing with a puzzle and a parent comes into the room and calls her name, she can shift attention from the puzzle to her parent. Children on the autism spectrum have difficulty making that attention shift regardless of whether they are engaged with a preferred item or not.

Children who are developing normally learn language when we provide language for them that matches their attention or where they are looking. If a child sees a dog and a parent says "dog!" the child learns to associate the word "dog" with the animal in front of him or her. The parent's language is contingent, meaning that the parent provides language that matches the child's focus. However in our daily activities we often do not overlay language exactly at the right moment. Typical children have the ability to shift attention quickly to match the parent's focus of attention. For example, if a child and her father are out for a walk and he sees a balloon in the sky, he points to the balloon for his daughter to see and then exclaims "balloon!" The child with autism may not look at where her father is pointing and may remain focused on whatever she was looking at before. Thus she did not process or learn the label for "balloon."

Lack of Interest

Your child isn't interested in where you want them to look. Children on the autism spectrum are often focused on something else that they consider more interesting. Indeed, they are often completely focused on what is interesting only to them. Shifting their attention to a social stimulus (your calling their name) doesn't come naturally to them or isn't motivating for them. This is related to social development in that typical children are interested in a variety of things, and often share our interests.

Children on the autism spectrum can have a restricted range of interests that often don't match ours. So they are less motivated to respond to us. This impacts their language development because they attend to our language much less than a typical child does.

Processing Difficulties

Some children on the autism spectrum have difficulty processing specific language when there are background sounds. They cannot filter out the non-relevant sounds and attend to the relevant language. The result is that it all becomes noise because the child has difficulty with auditory processing. Other children may have difficulty with what is simply called language processing. These children often take longer than what would be expected to respond to language. A speech and language therapist may be able to determine if your child has difficulty with auditory or language processing. Both types of processing difficulties are treatable.

Missing Nonverbal Cues

Children with autism also have difficulty following our nonverbal social language. A typical child uses all nonverbal and verbal communication available to her; the child with autism does not. For example, if mom points to her child's cup and says "Susan, get your cup," the typical child follows her mom's point and uses any language understanding to figure out that mom wants her to get the cup. The child with autism often misses the nonverbal cues; she may not follow her mom's gaze or her point towards the cup.

These are some of the reasons why children on the autism spectrum do not respond to you or follow your directions. Think about the type of language that your child is learning. Many children on the autism spectrum learn language for things that interest them or for items they want. Usually these are things that motivate them.

This may be difficult to accept. However, children can change if we know what to teach and how to teach. The next section explains what you can do to help your child better understand language.

STRATEGIES FOR CHANGE

Join Your Child's Attention

First, let's think about attention. **Your child is more likely to access your language if you provide language that overlaps where she is already looking**. This is called contingent language. For example if your child is pushing a car, get down on your child's level and say "car." Don't try to get your child to look at you because you are then asking her to shift her attention, which is difficult for her, and she is less likely to match your label "car" with her toy because she is not looking at her car anymore. So the first thing to remember is to match the focus of your child's attention. Don't try to change your child's focus, instead join her, and then label the item that has her attention.[1] This is an effective strategy which would be considered more of a developmental approach rather than a behavioral one.

Use Simple Language

Contrary to how we might speak to a typically developing child, **your child will learn language faster if you keep your language simple**. If your child is not yet talking, communicate with one word only ("cup", "car"). If your child is already using one word utterances, then communicate using one and two words, ("train go", "bye baby"). As her language develops continue to use two word phrases, slowly progress to using three words and so on. Maximize your child's language learning by limiting your language to her level. Too many words can slow down learning.

Nouns First

When you provide a label that matches your child's focus, try to make it a noun ("crayon"), instead of "draw." Once your child understands approximately 50 nouns, then you can begin to label using verbs ("push car") or adjectives ("big car").

Use Consistent Language

Your child will learn with lots of repetition. Provide the same language over and over for your child. It is reasonable to label "ball" 15 times a day. That is how the word "ball" will be associated with the toy. You will have plenty of opportunities to do this, because if you match your attention to your child's, you will capture what she is interested in. This is a powerful technique because your child is much more likely to learn language for the things that interest her.

Use Visual Cues

Let's move on to situations that are more challenging. You cannot match your child's interests all day long, and nor should you have to. There will be many times when you need to get your child's attention to participate in activities that are not of interest to her. What then?

If you want your child's attention, get down to her level, put your face very close to her, and make eye-contact. You may need to gently guide her face (touch her cheek or under her chin) to get her to look at you, or close to looking at you, and you may need to wait and persist for her to respond. This is key if you want her to give you her attention. When you have her attention, the next step is to use as little language as possible to get your message across. Most **children on the autism spectrum will respond much better to your requests if you give them some advance preparation time**. Therefore before you expect her to respond, give her a warning ("Get ready, bath time.") If you are unsure of whether your child understands you, then it is extremely effective to show her a picture of what will happen next. Show your child a photograph of the bathtub at the same time that you give her the "get ready" warning. The idea is to keep your communication as simple and concrete as possible ("Get ready pizza.") Then give your child a visual cue (the photo) to help her understand what is coming next. Pairing your language with the photo can also assist her to learn what activity goes with the word "bath time." Then after a minute or so, and at an appropriate time (after she has turned the last page of a book, or completed a puzzle, or pushed a car to the end of the rug), communicate your instruction a second time. Again, get down to your child's level, get her to look towards you (prompt her to look if necessary), and give her the photo again of "bathtime." Then follow through with your direction. Maybe she will go by herself, or take her by the hand, or if needed pick her up. She may be unhappy about the situation but you will have done all you can to get her to understand what you want. Any unhappiness on her part at this point is much less likely to be about not understanding, it is more likely to be about not wanting to change activity.

In the clinic we routinely use photos throughout the day for young children who do not show an understanding of language. Even if they do show some understanding, but it is inconsistent, or it is unclear to what extent they understand, we use a photo of the upcoming activity paired with our language. For example we use a photo of the snack table to transition a child from play on the floor to snack and a photo of the speech therapist to transition a child from a teacher to the speech therapist. You as parents can use them for every major activity (dinner, bath, bed) that happens throughout the day. Photos are effective as they help your child understand what is coming next and they anchor language to something visual and concrete. The more children understand, and the more they know what is coming next, the less likely they are to resist or tantrum. Visual cues and photos are used in a variety of different intervention approaches, for example the TEEACH approach (mentioned in chapter 9).

This may seem daunting, or you may be thinking that it is odd pulling out these photos all day long. You may feel it does not suit your lifestyle and home. I know that a clinic environment is very different and easier to structure than a busy home environment. However, take this knowledge, use elements that make sense for your needs, and try it with a few photos that you use at specific times. That is a completely acceptable compromise. For those of you who do try this photo strategy and like it, there are numerous ways to make the photos easily accessible when you need them at home or when out. You can keep the photos in a small plastic zip lock bag in your purse or bag, save them in your phone or in a digital key chain picture frame, or use pictures available online. Another idea is to mount a board up high somewhere central in your home (like a kitchen shopping list board) and keep the photos up there. You can use magnets or apply velcro to the back of the photos. That way you can pull off a photo whenever you need it.

It is surprising how fast children learn when we apply the strategies discussed above. They are powerful tools to change how you communicate with your child. Use them to jumpstart your child's ability to learn and understand language.

KEY POINTS

- There can be several reasons why your child is not responding to language: motivation, difficulty following multiple cues, difficulty shifting attention.

- Match your language to your child's focus of attention. For example, if your child is playing with a ball, get down on your child's level and say "ball".

- Keep your language and instructions concrete, simple and the same.

- Prepare your child in advance for your direction. Use a photo of the upcoming activity (e.g. her bed) and say "get ready, night night".

- Use a photo paired with your language to maximize your child's understanding of your directions. For example, show your child a photo of the bathtub when you are talking about taking a bath.

PERSONAL NOTES

4 FOUNDATIONS OF LANGUAGE

In chapter 3 we discussed why children on the autism spectrum may not pay attention to language or readily follow your gestures and nonverbal communication. We covered several intervention techniques that help the child on the autism spectrum to learn and understand language. This chapter provides you with strategies to develop your child's intentional communication and lay the path for language.

TYPICAL CHILDREN

Infants generally begin to babble playfully between 7 months and a year of age. Around the same time they begin to use simple gestures (e.g. wave bye), use sounds to join in familiar songs, try to mimic sounds, and reply vocally when called by name. By 13-18 months children approximate words to sing along with familiar songs. They combine words and gestures to get their desires met, and greet familiar people with their versions of "hi" or "bye." Beginning at around a year of age, children begin to say single words. By 18 months they usually have approximately 50 words. At this stage their language learning speeds up considerably and parents witness a word burst. They begin to repeat words heard in conversation, and by their second birthday children are using two word phrases "mommy gone." Between two and half and three years of age children combine 3 or 4 words in spontaneous speech. They also begin to answer "what" and "where" questions.

CHILDREN ON THE AUTISM SPECTRUM

In contrast to the description above you may find that you are often doing everything you can to guess at what your child wants. Sometimes you get it right but often you do not, and your child becomes increasingly frustrated sometimes escalating into a tantrum. Many parents hold one object after another in front of their child hoping that they stumble on to what it is their child wants. This scenario usually occurs because your child cannot effectively communicate, and you cannot read his or her mind. Nor should you have to. Parents usually assume that their child is having difficulty communicating because his or her spoken language hasn't yet developed or is delayed. Of course this is one major aspect of the problem. But it isn't the only cause. In the following three sections I draw your attention to the critical, yet often overlooked, role of gestures in communication which are an integral part of the foundation for learning language. I highlight three reasons why gestures affect communication in young children on the autism spectrum: they use gestures infrequently; they do not know how to use gestures for attention; and the quality of their gestures is lacking or unclear.

Infrequent Gestures

Children on the autism spectrum use gestures much less than typical children do, and when they do use gestures, the communicative quality of those gestures can be lacking. I am referring to gestures that are directly communicative, for example giving and pointing. Typical children use these gestures for many different reasons. They may gesture to request help or to get their needs met. For example, Johnny gives his juice to mom for her to open it. Or he brings his toy truck to dad because the wheel is stuck. Or when dad asks, "What do you want?" he points to the bag of crackers. There are other types of descriptive gestures that also clearly convey meaning. Think of how many two year olds you have seen raising their arms for mom or dad to pick them up. Their intention is clear, "Pick me up!"

Typical children use a variety of these gestures by about 20 months of age. Children not only communicate verbally but nonverbal communication also plays a key role as well. Your child may not be using these types of gestures to make his/her requests. If your child is not yet using spoken language to communicate and he is not using gestures as he should, it is not surprising that you are playing a guessing game.

Gestures for Attention

Even if your child is using gestures, the quality of those gestures may not be quite like that of the typical child. This matters because the quality can greatly contribute to how effectively a child communicates. Most of the children I see do not know how to get someone's attention. They don't know that they can tap someone's arm to get their attention before they ask for a cookie. Or make sure that dad is looking when they ask for help with a puzzle. Or wait till mom is facing them before they ask for "up". They make their request, but the person who is supposed to be the recipient of their communication has no idea that the child has just tried to communicate to them. The result is that the child becomes very frustrated and tantrums. Or feels helpless and gives up. Both are undesirable outcomes. As a first step just knowing when and how to get someone's attention can result in success or frustrating failure.

Unclear Gestures

Next, how your child uses his/her gestures can make a difference. It should be very clear where your child is pointing. Many children on the autism spectrum partially gesture or use incomplete gestures. Their point may not be fully formed, or instead of giving an item with a clearly directed outstretched arm towards a person, they may thrust the object in the general direction of the person. When this occurs the intention of the gesture is more difficult to read.

Summary

Nonverbal communication plays a large role in how we communicate. **Developing your child's ability to use gestures effectively will give him a means to clearly show his intentions**. When children see the power of their communication (be it nonverbal or verbal) they become motivated to communicate more. When that happens, you have gold.

STRATEGIES FOR CHANGE

Many children come into our clinic with little or no functional communication. They have no means to express what they want or don't want. Instead you play a guessing game. Or they may use your hand as a tool and lead you to what they want; often a tantrum is what tells you that you didn't get it right. In this section you will learn how to teach your child to independently request the items he wants. In the process you will use several important teaching strategies: how to teach using the basics of discrete trial training, how to prompt effectively, how to motivate your child, how to strengthen weak skills and how to make sure your child's communication is social. These are essential teaching strategies that you will use repeatedly to teach many other skills. Most importantly, however, you will not only teach your child how to communicate, you will teach your child the power of communication, and jumpstart him on the pathway to speech.

The Pathway to Talking

I would not be surprised if you told me that your single most important goal is for your child to talk. That is because I cannot remember a parent who did not express language as their main concern. I recognize that this section is of enormous importance to parents and I hope to provide you with effective strategies to get your child on the pathway to talking.

Most parents think that the most direct route is to immediately work on your child's verbal language. However what you may not realize is that your child does not understand why he or she should talk. Many children on the autism spectrum do not understand what communication is and why they should care about it. Before your child will talk, he needs to want to. Therefore **the first step is for your child to understand the value of communication, that when he communicates with others he will get something in return**. If you want your child to talk, you must first teach him the power of communication. Second, **your child must learn to imitate others**. This is a basic prerequisite to language. Throughout this book you will see that imitation should be an essential part of your child's learning. For this reason chapter 7 is entirely devoted to imitation.

In the section below you will learn how to teach your child to communicate and to feel empowered by new skills.

The first skill your child will learn is how to make an "I want" request. We will cover three teaching strategies that will help you accomplish this goal: errorless learning; ensuring generalization; and how to progress from gestures to language.

Then we will build on "I want" by teaching a second skill: point to request. The three subsections under point to request cover additional teaching strategies that will help you and your child to achieve success: strengthen unstable learning; making a choice; and how to ensure your child's requests are communicative.

"I Want"

We begin by teaching your child to request desired items with the gesture for "I want". **A gesture will be much easier for your child to learn than trying to get him to immediately communicate using speech**. This is a powerful place to begin as your child will quickly learn that he can use communication to get what he wants. The "I want" gesture will be immediately rewarding to him and he will be motivated to communicate more as he learns how to use it for his wants and needs. I know many of you will be wondering if the gesture will slow down his speech, that if you teach him how to gesture he may not be motivated to talk. The answer is no. **Your child will become increasingly excited about communication and more motivated than ever to learn new and different ways to communicate.**

The "I want" gesture is a simple tap-tap on the chest (palm down) using the dominant hand. Every time your child wants something, if he is right handed, take his right hand and press it gently against his chest twice. At the same time, verbally say "I want." Then immediately give him the desired item. When you say "I want" you are using several important strategies. You are acknowledging your child's communication which signals to him that his communication was effective. You are providing the appropriate language that can replace the ("I want") gesture and modeling how to use it. By saying "I want" every time your child uses the gesture you are repeatedly exposing him to the language he can use. Please note that this is not meant to be sign language; rather consider it an easy way to pair a gesture with words.

Errorless Learning

It is important that you completely help your child to do this in the beginning. He will also learn much faster if you are consistent. Therefore every time your child wants something, prompt him to use the "I want" gesture. This is a very easy gesture that most children will learn to do over time. However, children learn at different rates. Some will learn to do this in a few days, others will take longer. The key is to keep prompting your child (doing the full action for him until he begins to get the idea). It is also important not to delay giving him the item after he completes the "I want" action because you want him to learn that the moment he initiates the "I want" gesture, he gets the item. Any delay weakens the association between the "I want" gesture and receiving the item.

After you have given full prompts for a few days, try testing to see if you can give a little less help. Do this by taking your child's hand and guiding it towards his chest, but see if he will complete the tap-tap on his own. One tap is also acceptable. The reason we use a double tap is because one tap can be ambiguous and easily missed. As you are guiding your child, if you feel him initiating part of the action, it is time to slowly decrease your prompt. Provide only the degree of prompting that he needs to complete the gesture. Your objective is to provide the right balance between allowing him an opportunity to independently initiate as much as possible and still successfully complete the gesture. Therefore continue to give as much help as is needed for him to successfully make the request using "I want." You can also model the gesture for your child. To do this, you would enact the tap-tap gesture on yourself essentially providing an example, or a model, of what he should do. Your child should then imitate you and complete the gesture on himself. The goal however, is to slowly reduce your prompts until your child is completing the entire gesture independently. This process can take days and for some children, several weeks. Proceed only as fast as your child learns. Try not to decrease your prompts too quickly. However do not worry if you misjudge your child's pace and fade your prompts too rapidly. If this happens reevaluate and provide your child with as much help as he needs. This is called errorless learning.

The concept behind **errorless learning** is that when you begin to teach your child something, you are starting from the very beginning. He doesn't know what you want, or expect. Therefore you have to begin with only one very specific, simple and clear goal, just as we did with "I want." Then provide as much help as your child needs to get it right. To do this you will use a **hierarchy of prompts**. First you will provide hand-over-hand prompting. In the example of "I want," you will take your child's hand and completely guide it from beginning to end to make the tap-tap gesture. Another term for a hand-over-hand prompt is a full physical prompt. Then you can test to see if you can pull back, so that you are only giving a partial physical prompt. Thereafter remain consistent with giving the same partial prompt (and no more) every time. You should not prompt any more than necessary. You can provide a partial prompt in a variety of ways. For example you can guide your child's hand to his chest and then let go for him to complete the tap-tap or you can touch his elbow as a minimal cue (and provide no more help than that). Be comfortable with the idea that there are different ways to partially prompt which also provide different degrees of help. You can prompt any way that works for you and your child. There is no "right" way. However, remember to always pair your prompt with language, in this example it would be "I want". The idea though is to gradually decrease how much you prompt until your child can complete your teaching goal independently. Errorless learning is critical because it not only avoids learning the wrong thing but also avoids the frustration of making mistakes.

Ensure Generalization

The next question is whether your child is initiating a request in the same way with other people in the family. Often what happens is that a child learns a new skill with one person, or in one situation, and does not learn to use it flexibly (i.e. with different people, in different environments, with different objects). This is called generalization; the ability to use a skill in generalized situations (and not just a specific one). Of course as you may realize, the problem with this is that in real life we use our skills and knowledge in many different situations. The more we can adapt, the better we cope.

If your child hasn't generalized using "I want," your next step is to focus on this. Do it in exactly the same way you started teaching the skill, except now it will be with a different person, or at grandma's house, or in the park. Even if your child was initiating "I want" independently with you, it is possible that when you attempt to generalize it with a new person, the new person may have to prompt the skill. Typically, your child should require a much shorter period of prompting before using it independently in a new context.

A preemptive approach is to have multiple people expect the "I want" gesture from your child at the outset. The benefit is greater intensity (i.e. your child will have to practice it much more often), probably resulting in quicker learning, and built in generalization from the start. This may be made easier by having periodic family meetings where you essentially communicate "This is what I'm working on with him this week, and this is how we do it."

From Gestures to Language

The exciting possibility is that you may find that as your child becomes increasingly competent at using the "I want" gesture, he or she may start to verbalize something that sounds like "I want". This is a direct result of your providing the language "I want" every time he or she makes the tap-tap gesture. In this case you encounter the exciting dilemma of whether to acknowledge the tap-tap gesture or whether to acknowledge the verbalization that may be far from perfect.

The important thing to remember is that you should acknowledge any attempt at appropriate communication. If your child makes any kind of verbalization as he enacts the tap-tap gesture, give your child the item he requested and model the language "I want" as you give it to him. If your child approximates a verbalization of "I want" instead of using the tap-tap gesture, you should immediately accept the verbal approximation. Respond by providing a model of how it should sound, i.e., "I want", model the tap-tap on yourself as you do this and then immediately give your child the item he requested. You should not make your child practice saying "I want" to get a clearer request, nor should you insist that he use the gesture before receiving the desired item. Accept any verbal approximation immediately and just model "I want".

Only a small percentage of children begin to verbalize this quickly. It is much more likely that your child will need to become competent at using a variety of gestures and learn to imitate several actions before he will to try to talk.

Point to Request

The next step will be to teach your child to make a more specific request by pointing to the item that he wants. Now when he initiates the "I want" sign, hold up the desired item with one hand, and with your other hand, form his index finger into a point. Prompt the point using the same hand that he used for "I want." Most young children who come into our clinic need hand-over-hand prompting at first. As I explained in the previous section this means you should assume he has no idea what you want. Help him completely to form his finger into a point and prompt him to point to the item that he wants. Then label the item he has requested (and is pointing to) and immediately give it to him. Here is an example: Jimmy comes into the kitchen, looks at his cup on the counter and signs "I want" with his right hand. Mom immediately acknowledges his communication and provides a verbal model for him by saying "I want", then she takes his right hand and fully prompts him to point at the cup. As she does so, she says "cup" (you could say "juice," "milk" or "drink," whichever is meaningful for your child), and gives it to him. Remember to keep your language very simple, just one word at this time.

Similar to your teaching for the "I want" gesture, continue prompting your child to form the "point" providing as much help as he needs. Then as you feel him starting to initiate any portion of the point on his own, test if you can slightly decrease your prompt so that you are providing a partial physical prompt. Determine exactly what your child requires to be successful. Find the balance where you provide just enough assistance to complete the point but not too much to stifle emerging independence. Again, there are also different ways to provide a partial prompt. Here are some examples on how to partially prompt a point after the "I want" gesture:

- Your child reaches toward the item and you shape his hand into the point. Your child started the point by reaching out, then you finished it by shaping the point (this is a considerable partial prompt).

- Your child reaches toward the item and makes his hand into a fist - you shape his hand into the point (this is a partial prompt).

- You guide your child's arm so that it is extended towards the object, then he makes the point himself (this is a lesser prompt).

- Your child extends his arm, makes his hand into a fist and approximates a point (it is a really close approximation but the point is not fully formed) - you help him to form his point properly (this is a small partial prompt).

- After your child signs for "I want," you touch his hand and then he forms the point on his own (this is still a small partial prompt because he needed a little tap reminder to follow through and make the point).

These examples demonstrate how you can begin with a bigger partial prompt and then decrease to a lesser partial prompt by giving your child less and less help to form the point. You will have to judge when you think you can pull back completely and push your child towards independence. However make sure he is consistently pointing with a partial physical prompt before you consider pulling back. Then when you think your child is approaching independence, pull back once and evaluate what happens. There is no harm in doing this as long as you aren't doing it so often that you are compromising the errorless learning we talked about earlier. If he does point independently - terrific! If not, stay resolute and continue to provide those faded physical prompts for a while, then test again to determine if he can do it by himself. Lastly, make sure your child now uses his new skill not only with you, but with all members of the family, and in different places.

Strengthen Unstable Learning

This section highlights another key strategy. Anytime you need to provide more prompting, do it! I know it is probably the last thing you will want to do, but it is worth it in the long run. **It is fairly common to see unstable learning in young children on the autism spectrum.** I mean that they are independently using a newly learned skill, then suddenly they seem a little shaky and aren't as independent as they were before. You wait them out in the hope that they will demonstrate the skill, but you end up having to prompt them. If you find yourself in this situation (most of you will at some time or another), don't hesitate to reevaluate and provide more prompting immediately. With preemptive action you will prevent the skill from slipping even further, and instead strengthen the learning with some extra prompting. Usually this yields fast results, and before long the child is back to demonstrating the skill independently.

Making a Choice

Now you are in a position to really use the point to help you. Parents often have a difficult challenge determining what their child wants. You know your child wants something but you can't figure out what it is. So you offer item after item until you finally find the right one. This is incredibly frustrating for you and your child. The pointing gesture gives both of you a wonderful mechanism to increase the likelihood that your child can successfully communicate his request. Once he is pointing independently to request for a desired item, the next step is to introduce two items.

Imagine that Jimmy comes into the kitchen, there are several items on the counter, and he signs "I want." Now you can hold up two of the items and he can indicate his preference by pointing. If he does not point spontaneously in this context, determine which one he looks towards (usually the item he wants), then prompt him to point to that item. He will soon be pointing with ease to make a choice.

Usually at this stage children have learned the power of the point. They use it throughout the day in a variety of situations to request for items both near and far. For example, Jimmy enters the kitchen and points to the closet above the counter where he knows mom keeps the cookies. It empowers children enormously and makes your life much easier. Your child has a means to communicate what he wants and the quality of your interactions changes for the better. This is huge step forward.

Make It Communicative

There is another important component to successful communication. When we ask someone for something we usually look at them. Your child should learn to include eye-contact with his gesture. His intention to communicate will be clear and **eye-contact contributes to the quality of successful communication**. Many children on the autism spectrum learn to point, but they remain overly focused on the item they are trying to obtain and barely look at another person as they make the request. When your child requests something it should feel social. You are just as important as the item he is trying to get, so he needs to include you in his communication.

You may be wondering just how you will achieve this goal. It is straightforward. Every time your child points to make a request, you need to wait. Contrary to what you have done before, you will not jump in right away and honor the communication. Rather, you are going to expect your child to look at you before you give him the item. Waiting can be a powerful tool. The challenging part is determining just how long to wait to see if your child will independently look at you, or if you need to help him with a little prompt. Regardless, the moment he makes eye-contact coordinated with the point, immediately follow through just as you did before. Let's use the previous example: Jimmy comes into the kitchen, looks at his cup on the counter, signs "I want" and points to his cup. Mom stands close to him and looks at Jimmy expectantly (this is the wait). He hesitates, then points again and looks briefly at mom. Mom immediately exclaims "I want cup!" and gives it to him.

Of course you are wondering what you should do if your wait does not facilitate eye-contact. You already know the answer ... prompt for it. If you do need to prompt, gently touch your child under his chin and see if he will make eye-contact. If not, take his chin and gently turn his head towards you. Position your face very close to his face until he makes eye-contact, even if it is brief. Then prompt him the same way every time the opportunity arises. Don't be tempted to use the wait only; he may need your assistance initially. If you progress too quickly you may be inadvertently setting him up for frustration. However after practicing with a prompt for a period of time, consider checking again to determine if he can spontaneously initiate eye-contact when you wait.

As you can see in the above example there are several strategies you can use to make your wait effective. First, make sure you are in close physical proximity to your child. It will be easier for him to coordinate his attention between you and the item he wants. Second, exaggerate your facial expressions. In that moment when you are waiting, you should be looking expectantly at your child's face, obviously waiting for him to do something. Then, when your child does make eye-contact, everything about you should be highly positive. Your expression should immediately change to a big smile, your voice should be animated, make physical contact with your child (caress him affectionately, kiss his cheek, or ruffle his hair, whatever your child enjoys). Your response is important because it strengthens the social quality of the communication exchange.

LEARNING CAN CHANGE

You learned several specialized teaching techniques in this chapter: how to successfully prompt a new skill from acquisition to independence, how to ensure a skill is generalized, and how to maintain newly acquired skills. These are elements of discrete trial training; they are fundamental to successful teaching for young children on the autism spectrum.

I anticipate that at this point you may be experiencing some mixed feelings. On the one hand you are excited about teaching strategies that work. On the other hand, many parents experience a sense of desperation regarding how much they have to change their everyday interactions in order for their child to learn. However I would be remiss if I did not emphasize that many young children on the autism spectrum need this level of very specialized teaching at the outset to jumpstart their learning. However your child's learning will change. **Over time you will see him begin to learn from his natural environment.** You will recognize the change because he will demonstrate knowledge that you did not teach him. It's an incredibly exciting time when that begins to happen. At that point you can consider gradually reducing the specialized teaching. The goal will be for your child to increasingly learn from the natural environment. I have seen this transition occur in many young children who came into our clinic needing highly specialized teaching at the beginning. Stay resolute, your child's learning will change. A heavy involvement of your time now, will pay off in having to invest much less time later!

KEY POINTS

- If you want your child to talk, you must first teach him or her why communication is valuable.

- Gestures are critical for effective nonverbal communication.

- To begin, teach "I want". Prompt as much as necessary first, then fade your prompts, remember to give the desired item immediately.

- Next work on pointing to request, first with one item, then building in choice. Use errorless learning, use a prompt hierarchy, and temporarily provide increased prompting if the point needs strengthening.

- Make sure each newly acquired skill is generalized (used with different people and in different places).

- Require eye-contact; it is an important social aspect of communication. Wait before you acknowledge your child's communication, it is a powerful technique to elicit eye-contact.

- Initially your child needs specialized teaching to jumpstart the learning process.

- Your child needs predictability, repetition, and consistency.

- Over time your child's learning will change; it will become spontaneous as it is for typical children.

PERSONAL NOTES

5 DEVELOPING SOCIAL INTERACTIONS

How can I get my child to laugh and have fun with me and others? Many parents express this concern as the relationship between you and your child goes to the core of being a parent. Parents often report that their child does not notice if they came into the room or if they leave. They yearn for an excited welcome hug and pleas to play when they return from work. They feel that their child is preoccupied in his own interests and only communicates when he needs something. On the first day in the clinic we ask parents about their goals. Nearly all say they want their child to look at them, to communicate and interact socially, and to play with other children.

The ability to engage in social relationships is an important core area of development that needs to be directly targeted for children on the autism spectrum. You will use simple yet powerful techniques in the context of social baby games. I will explain what to do and why it is so effective.

TYPICAL CHILDREN

By social baby games I mean peek-a-boo, itsy bitsy spider (or any easy songs with accompanying actions), and tickle games ("I'm going to ... get you!") These types of games are suitable for very young children. Typical children between 6 and 10 months return a smile and begin to play peek-a-boo. Essentially we are going to replicate what parents do instinctively with their babies every day. Think of mom or dad changing the baby's diaper. Baby is on her back. Mom begins the game. She leans over her baby, holds out her arms, makes her face very animated and her voice high pitched and excited "I'm going to ...." Her arms swoop down and in an exaggerated fashion she pretends that she is going to tickle her baby - except that halfway, she pauses and looks for her baby's reaction. Baby gives a big smile in return;

her eyes locked on her mom, she vocalizes and starts excitedly waving her arms and feet in anticipation. Mom responds "get you!" then finishes the swoop and tickles her. Both laugh together, sharing the fun and excitement of the moment and the tickle game. They do this a few times until it all becomes too much for the baby and she looks away. Mom is sensitive to her baby's reaction, she pauses and waits. After a while baby looks back at mom, kicks her legs and waves her arms, and mom resumes the tickle game.

On the surface these interactions seem simple. At their core however, they are powerfully social. Mom and baby become closely connected. They watch each other's faces; they laugh together, and share the enjoyment of the moment. It is a context where the baby can develop what we call **emotional contagion**, almost like catching another person's emotions. Mom gets excited; baby catches her emotions and becomes excited. It also happens the other way round, baby gets excited and mom responds to her by becoming highly affective (smiling, talking in an animated voice). It is reciprocal; mom tickles, baby laughs, mom waits, baby kicks her legs and waves her arms in anticipation, so mom tickles. It is a highly **shared social experience**. In the mental space between parent and child develops the beginnings of what we call intersubjectivity, or understanding another person.

Typical children are quite interactive in this context. They will hold their parents gaze for an extended period. At around 10 months of age infants begin to imitate their parent's actions in these routine games and they sometimes start the game. They cover their face to initiate peek-a-boo, they hold up their hands during the itsy bitsy spider song. Infants become more active social partners as they respond, reciprocate and initiate the actions and easy sounds associated with social games. In a 10 minute interaction typically developing children imitate on average 2 actions every minute.

CHILDREN ON THE AUTISM SPECTRUM

Even though your child is no longer an infant, it makes sense that we start here, with simple social games that parents play with their infants at around 6 months of age. You may have been trying to engage your child this way. However, many parents of children on the autism spectrum give up because they do not get the same feedback that parents of typical children receive. The child on the autism spectrum may not look at you, may not laugh with you, most likely will not let you know that he or she wants more. It is not easy to keep on playing games like these when your child does not show enjoyment. It is not surprising and understandable that many parents soon stop these interactions.

Most likely your child feels uncomfortable looking at your face. For him or her it is complex and your face is not easy to understand. Please do not take this personally. It has nothing to do with your parenting and how you interact with your child. Rather your child's brain processes faces differently than that of a child who is typically developing[1]. Typical children are comfortable looking at other people's faces. They want regular social attention and interaction; and faces meet their needs. However children on the autism spectrum often have different needs. For example, they may be preoccupied with seeking sensory input (see chapter 8). Therefore, apart from not 'reading' faces well, your child may not be motivated by them.

Your first goal is to **develop your child's ability to engage with you in social baby games**. These are also referred to as face-to-face dyadic interactions. The word dyad means two. In this context visualize you and your child face-to-face, nothing else. No objects, no toys, no other person. Why? From chapter 3 we know that children on the autism spectrum can become easily overloaded if we expect them to pay attention to too many things at once. Dyadic interactions make it easier for your child to stay focused on you. We do not want your child to have to shift attention between you and a toy, or between two people, or between your face and anything else. That would be setting your child up for an overload on her attention which is exactly what we want to avoid.

I hope you will be excited by the easy intervention strategies that follow. The first two strategies help you decide where and how you will begin. These will be important in setting you and your child up for success. The next seven strategies provide you with a step-by-step guide on how to develop face-to-face games that are not only fun, but that develop your child as an active social partner. They are: exaggerating your enthusiasm; making it predictable; using simple language; building anticipation; being contingent; changing the routine; and lastly, expanding your child's experience.

STRATEGIES FOR CHANGE

What Motivates Your Child

Start with one song that contains something interesting or motivating for your child. Perhaps it contains numbers, or maybe your child likes tickles. If you are at a loss for what song or game she will like, then think about whether your child engages in unusual behaviors that give her some type of sensory input. For example if your child likes to spin objects or spin herself, she is seeking visual input. If your child likes to crash her body into things she may be seeking what we call proprioceptive input (sensations we get from our joints and muscles). Our goal is to give your child that same input in a different way through social interaction. Think about a song or game that could provide the type of sensory stimulation that you child enjoys. For example, if your child crashes into things, a song that includes deep squeezes on her arms and legs may be a good starting point. Or for a child who is seeking visual input, a song like itsy bitsy spider may be a good choice as it contains lots of visually interesting movements. Not surprisingly, many different treatment approaches consider motivation to be essential to a child's success. For example Pivotal Response Training (mentioned in chapter 9) uses motivation in strategic ways to teach children in the natural environment.

Plan for Success

Once you have decided on your game or song, think about when you are going to try it. It will have to be a time when you can keep your child fairly structured and contained. This means that you can physically keep her present without squirming away or engaging in a different activity. This should not be a time when she has a choice. One idea might be similar to the example above, when you are changing her diaper, or while she is in the bath tub, or maybe after a bath when she is lying face up on the bed. Many parents take the opportunity to play interactive games when their child is in a stroller or in their high chair. Those are excellent times when your child is naturally in a position to be structured. Decide on your game and where to play it.

Now let's talk about your expectations and about your actions. When we start, many children on the autism spectrum don't react at all. They may mildly resist, many have a neutral affect (a serious face), and they don't participate in any of the actions, indicate enjoyment, or communicate for more. I want you as a parent to know that we see children like this all the time. These initial unresponsive reactions are common. I don't want any parent to think that their child isn't ready for this, that they can't do it. They are. So what are the implications for you? How should you begin to intervene?

Exaggerate Your Enthusiasm

Position yourself physically very close to your child. Your faces should be no more than 2 feet apart and at the same level. You are going to interact with high affect. This means all of your **expressions need to be exaggerated,** what would be considered over the top. You are going to be highly enthusiastic and excited in your facial expressions and in your voice. You will help your child to physically engage in the actions so that she is participating with you even if you are doing all the work. You are going to be highly reinforcing, no matter how much you help your child, or how neutral her affect. This means you will clap for her, praise her excitedly, cheer "hooray!" or anything else you can think of. Remember that a mere "good Sophie" in a boring voice will not suffice. You need to be excited and you need to show it. These are the key strategies to remember.

You may be wondering why you need to be so animated, excited, and overly positive. We use this approach in the clinic and consistently find that young children respond extremely well. Slowly they change from being serious little people with neutral affect to smiling children with bright engaged faces. If you look happy, you feel happy. If you feel happy, you enjoy your day. **Children (or anyone for that matter) who have a bright disposition are open to learning and new experiences**. I see enormous changes in children just by changing their affect. So it is one of the key areas of development that I begin with right away.

You may be thinking, fair enough, I'll be positive, but is it really necessary to exaggerate my affect? The answer is a resounding yes! Remember that for children on the autism spectrum it does not come naturally to look at our faces. Because of this, they often miss cues, our language, our expressions, and our feelings. Keep in mind that I am talking generally. Children are very different. Of course it is not all black and white. However to some degree these characteristics will apply to all children on the spectrum. Our goal is to give children a big jumpstart. Therefore in order for them to really pay attention to us, to attend to our language, to our changes in expression, to our positive emotions, and take it in, initially we must exaggerate it all. Be assured that this is not something your child will need in the long term. I am amazed every day at how little ones change. As they transform, our interactions change accordingly, until we are interacting naturally, just like we would with a typical child.

Make it Predictable

Predictability is essential. **Children on the autism spectrum have difficulty predicting situations and understanding what is going to come next**. This is partly because they don't read all of the subtle cues that will give them this information. To read these cues typical children carefully study our faces – our eyes, expressions, glances, body language and our gestures. They pay attention to a variety of cues in their environment that give them information about what might be coming next. You already know it is difficult for children on the autism spectrum to look at our faces and simultaneously pay attention to multiple stimuli. When they are not sure what is coming next or how a situation will unfold, children on the autism spectrum can become very anxious. Often we see their anxiety in the form of protests or tantrums.

What does this mean for you? When you play with your child, we want her to be comfortable. We want to prevent your child from becoming anxious because she doesn't know what is coming next. We want her to be able to anticipate how events will unfold and look forward to interacting with you. Therefore **build in predictability**. You achieve this by making your games routine. Resist changing your games daily. Keep them the same. Keep your language the same, keep your actions the same, keep the elements of the game consistent and highly predictable. For example if you play peek-a-boo and cover your face with your hands, the next time you play the game, use your hands again. Refrain from using a blanket, it will change the game. Or if you sing "Old McDonald" and start with the horse, then always start with the horse.

I know this may seem like you are setting your child up to learn in an inflexible way. However, it is only a starting point to set you and your child up for success. As you play these games more you can judge if you can change the game a little, or add something new. If your child responds positively, then go ahead and build in variety. Some children may not need so much predictability. Children are all different. In our clinic we work with every child according to his or her individual needs. There is no "one fits all" approach. Obviously in this book I cannot provide with you strategies that exactly match your child's learning. Rather I can guide you generally with essential strategies that are effective for most children. It will be up to you to decide how and when you apply the techniques. Regardless, I want you to have the knowledge so that you can adjust your interactions and your approach accordingly.

As I said before, **it may take a few weeks** for your child to begin to respond positively to these games. Most likely you will need lots of patience. Children on the autism spectrum often need a lot of repetition when we start to work with them. Hang in there. You should start to see change, even if in the beginning it is just a tiny little bit less resistance to being there with you than you saw the day before.

Use Simple Language

Let's talk about some other elements you can build into your games. First be mindful of your language. Keep it simple. This applies to games other than a song (peek-a-boo, for example). Use no more than one to two words at a time. Instead of saying "I'm going to get you" rather say "get you!" Instead of "First it is mommy's turn, then it will be Sophie's turn", rather say "First mommy, then Sophie!" Or, in place of "There you are!" simply say "Hi!"

Build Anticipation

Next, think about building in anticipation. In your tickle game, I want you to pause before you swoop in and tickle. Or make your fingers pretend to walk towards your child across the top of her high chair. Walk them slowly saying "going to ...", and pause. Look at your child for a reaction. Resume walking your fingers steadily towards your child, "going to ...," pause again. Slowly get closer to your child who is waiting with anticipation for that final tickle that really is going to get her. You are creating excitement, but also if your child is expecting the tickle, your pause creates a natural opportunity for her to pay attention to you, and to look at you, which is precisely what you want. Your objective is to **create opportunities that naturally elicit interaction** from your child. Pausing in key places in a routine game is an easy and powerful way to achieve this. Orchestrate the anticipation, accentuate your child's expectation and heighten the fun when the swoop actually occurs. Use these pauses to elicit eye-contact, affect (smiling, laughing), verbal language (an approximation of "tickle"), or maybe even sign language if it is already familiar to your child (the sign for "more"). Ultimately, precisely at the fun part, pause with a highly animated expression on your face, and wait. In that pause see if your child will look at you and use whatever means of functional communication they have to request that you resume the game. For example, if you are working on "I want" (see chapter 4), this is an excellent opportunity to prompt your child to enact the "I want" gesture as a request to continue the game.

Be Contingent

This is another way of saying stay in the moment with your child, **follow her initiation and attention**. If she laughs, you laugh with her. If she claps, clap with her. If she says "more", you follow up with "more tickles," then tickle her. Set up the game, and create opportunities for your child to respond. When she does, you need to be contingent. Why? Because that is where her attention is at that moment and you want to capitalize on her attention. Therefore stay with her focus and build on it. At that moment your child is open to learning and social interaction, go with it.

Change the Routine

After your child knows and enjoys a particular game, you can start to change a piece of the routine. Change it in a fun way so that your child will think it is funny. For example, if you are singing "Old McDonald", when you get to the cow part and you are supposed to make the "moo", come out with a ridiculous "oink" instead. Or if you are playing a tickle game, instead of swooping from above, tickle your child's legs under her high chair. These fun variations of what your child expects create ripe opportunities for your child to look at you, to share the excitement with you, and for you both to laugh together.

Expand the Experience

Build on your language. If you get to a point where your child is comfortable and have added new elements and new games, you can use the games to expand your language. For example instead of singing "Itsy Bitsy Spider" the usual way, sing a slightly different version in a deep voice "The big, big spider went ..." Change your actions slightly to match the big spider, put your arms out to show it is big. Here you have added a new word "big" and you have changed the routine slightly in a fun way that many children enjoy. As you can imagine, you can create several variations of the spider. Another fun variation is the baby spider (squeaky voice with tiny actions). Don't be tempted to change your language too much or to add too much language. Adding **one new word at a time** is enough to build on what you had before and introduce something new. At the same time you are having fun and developing shared social interactions.

PEOPLE ARE FUN

These beginning interactions are where we need to start. Other family members or a caregiver can help provide the predictability and repetition that your child needs. Trained therapists in the clinic use these techniques daily. It is too much to expect your child to be able to interact with other children if she is not yet consistently interacting with an adult. By developing these interactions you are laying the groundwork for social interactions with other children. Your child learns to watch you to see what you are going to do, but more importantly, your child learns to enjoy these interactions and she learns that other people are fun. This is critical. When you have achieved this your child will be more prepared to enjoy social interactions with other children.

KEY POINTS

- Face-to-face interactions are a powerful way to connect socially with your child.

- Use physical proximity and exaggerated affect. Be overly enthusiastic in your facial expressions and your voice.

- Include elements that are highly motivating for your child. For example, choose a song with hand motions for a child who seeks visual stimulation; consider a song that contains deep squeezes for a child who seeks strong body contact and pressure.

- Make it predictable.

- Keep your language simple.

- Use anticipation (pause to enhance the social expectation), be contingent (match your child's social actions), then slowly expand or change the routine.

PERSONAL NOTES

6 SHARING EXPERIENCES

In the previous chapter we talked about how to create fun face-to-face interactions. On the surface it appears simple. Underneath we are building a foundation for your child to interact with you purely for fun and not only when he wants something.

In this chapter we will take it a step further. What we want is for your child to **share the things that interest him with other people**. We will do this by progressing from face-to-face interactions to more advanced social interactions.

TYPICAL CHILDREN

John is in his high chair finishing dinner and Dad walks in the door. John looks from his mom to his dad and back to his mom again with a huge smile on his face. As if to say "look mom, dad's here!" In that simple interaction, without any language, John conveys to his mom that he is thrilled to see his dad. (I know this is a very stereotypical example. I hope that you can take it and reverse the parent roles.)

Here is another scenario. It is similar to the previous one except that now John looks from his mom to an object and back to mom again. They are out on a walk and a bus approaches. John loves buses! A big smile breaks over his face as he sees the bus, he turns to look at his mom with glee and points towards it as if to say "Look mom there's a bus! Do you see it too?" All he wants is to make sure that his mom shares his interest and delight at seeing the bus. When he looks from the bus to mom, and then back to the bus, it is called a shared look. It is a way of sharing experiences with others purely for enjoyment. We focus our attention on the same thing (person or object or activity) and share the experience together in a way that feels very connected. This is called **shared or joint attention**.

Indeed we are constantly sharing our thoughts, experiences, likes and dislikes, and our lives with others around us. We want to share because we are social. We accomplish this with language but we also use nonverbal means. Typical children do this naturally, using nonverbal gestures before they learn to talk. Joint attention skills, such as shared looks, pointing and showing emerge very early. Typical children begin to engage in shared looks when they are around 6 months old, they begin to show items of interest to us around 10 months, by 14 months they look at where we are pointing, and they point with clear communicative intent at around 16 months of age.

By two years of age typical children are constantly pointing out things and showing us things that delight them. Nobody teaches them to do this. It is just part of how they develop. The irony is that we take all of this for granted; we don't stop to think about it. That is until we have a little one, who we love dearly, who does not share his joy, discoveries, or experiences.

CHILDREN ON THE AUTISM SPECTRUM

I am always sensitive about the impact of information on parents. I know that you want me to be honest, and you want to help your child. But I also know that with knowledge comes a realization that perhaps this is more than you had bargained for. The truth is that social development does not occur naturally in children on the autism spectrum like it does in typical children. That is not easy to accept, but you have to be strong for your child, yourself, and your family.

We can teach children on the autism spectrum to engage in joint attention and share their experiences, joys, and interests. Once we show them how, they enjoy sharing their worlds with us and connecting with us. When they do you will treasure those moments. Also, just as in many other areas of your child's development, **what starts off having to be taught in the beginning becomes more and more natural over time**.

The change can be so significant that a stranger would never know that a child ever had difficulty engaging in joint attention.

Joint attention skills are wonderful tools to be social. However, there are also other reasons why joint attention is so important. It is one of the earliest areas that significantly impacts how children develop. We know that **joint attention is related to language**. Children who use joint attention skills when they are younger will develop better language as they get older[1-3]. Further early joint attention skills are related to more advanced social skills like being able to take another person's perspective. For these reasons joint attention is a very powerful area to target in young children. **If you teach it, you can change it**[4].

Using the strategies below you will learn to teach your child how to engage in joint attention using three different skills: shared looking; pointing; and showing.

There are two strategies that are very effective at eliciting shared looking: using routines; and incorporating surprise.

When you progress to teaching pointing and showing you will see that the teaching strategies for both of these skills are similar: first demonstrate or model the gesture; then prompt your child to point or show; and lastly you will require eye-contact with the gesture.

STRATEGIES FOR CHANGE

Shared Looks

William is pushing his brand new toy train across the floor. He pushes a button and to his surprise the train blows a whistle. He is thrilled! He breaks out in a big smile, looks at his dad and then looks back at his train to do it again. Two year old William just engaged in a shared look with his father. His quick look back at his dad had a clear purpose – to share how fun his train is. It was as if he said, "Wow dad!" Essentially, you want your child to include you in something they enjoy by looking from the object to you and then back to the object again. It sounds simple, but it is more difficult than purely face-to-face interactions because it requires the child to shift his attention between you and an object. Or shift his attention between you and another person. In this case William shifted his attention from the train to his father and back to the train.

This is one of the earliest joint attention skills that typical children spontaneously initiate. One year old infants often engage in shared looks with others. It is a good place for us to start as we can build on some of the strategies you used in the previous chapter. The way to get your child to engage in shared looks with you is via fun face-to-face interactions just as you learned to do in chapter 5, except now we are going to include objects.

Begin by setting up a fun interaction. Start almost in a face-to-face interaction. For example your child is lying on his back in the midst of a diaper change. The dirty diaper is off, your child is wiped clean and the next step is for the clean diaper to go on. Instead you slip a puppet on your hand, a duck for example. You lean over your child and just as we described in the previous chapter, you pretend to swoop in on your child with "I'm going to get you!" The duck swoops down and plants kisses on your child's belly. The first time you do this your child may laugh with delight. Now hold the duck back again (in position ready to swoop down) and pause. Exaggerate your enthusiasm. Your goal is to **create a sense of anticipation** and excitement at what is going to come next. You start with "I'm ..." and then pause. The **pause is your key strategy** because it is very likely at this point your child will engage in a shared look out of pure pleasure. He'll be looking at the duck that is about to swoop down on his belly, then he will glance at you with anticipation, then back to the duck to see what will happen. When your child does this you want him to see the excitement and enthusiasm on your face. The moment your child makes that shared look, swoop down and have the duck plant kisses all over his belly. If at any point you are not successful at eliciting a shared look, increase the excitement and anticipation. Hold the duck up high and add "going to ..." then pause, fake the beginning of a swoop. Anything to really build up anticipation in your child before the duck swoops in. At some point in the buildup your child will engage in a shared look with you. Celebrate the moment. You have achieved a lot.

Use Routines

Just as in face-to-face interactions (chapter 5), set your child up for the same games over and over again, so he knows what is coming next. The next day he sees the duck appear he will be excited because he enjoys the interaction and knows what to expect. As you use the same routines you will see more and more of those treasured shared looks.

Incorporate Surprise

As we discussed in chapter 5 also change your child's expectations. I will use a different example to illustrate this for you. Imagine you have set up a routine where you blow bubbles and pop them. Your child loves this activity, and expects several small bubbles to come out of the wand. The pleasure of the activity elicits shared looks from your child between you and the bubbles. Therefore, after several days, change it. Surprise your child. This time blow one long big bubble. Blow slowly so that it doesn't leave the wand for a while, and when it does it is much, much bigger than any you have blown before. It is the same activity but different than what your child expected. By slightly changing the routine you have created a new element of surprise that naturally creates an opportunity for your child to engage in joint attention with you.

Pointing

Another way for your child to share his experiences with you nonverbally is via pointing.   In chapter 4 we talked about teaching your child to make a request by pointing for what he wants. In that case the reason for your child's communication was to request. Here you are going to teach your child to point for a different reason; that is to share his experiences with you. The reason for using the point is important. When a child points to make a request he expects to obtain something or have a need met. When he points to share attention his reason is to share an experience with you.

For children on the autism spectrum **requesting is easier than joint attention** because requesting helps them meet their needs. Therefore it will be much easier to teach your child to point as a way to share experience if he can already point to make a request. If he is not yet pointing to make requests for desired items go back to chapter 4 and first teach your child to use a point to make requests.

However if your child is already independently pointing to request for what he wants (without any help from you), and making eye-contact with the requesting point (chapter 4), then you are ready to teach him how to point in a very social way – to share attention. You are going to use two methods – first you are going to be a role model, second you are going to prompt your child to point to share. Remember when you begin to teach a new skill your teaching will feel contrived and unnatural but as your child progresses from acquisition to mastery the interaction will gradually normalize.

Model Pointing

You are looking at a book with your child. Every time you point to a picture and your child follows your point to see the picture, you are modeling how to initiate a shared attention point. Further, you are jointly sharing the experience of looking at a book together. Be clear in your actions, engage with exaggerated affect and make it fun. Sound in awe of what you are both looking at together.

We can build on the earlier example of the approaching bus. The bus approaches, your child gives you that treasured shared look, and at that moment you respond with an excited "Yes, bus!" and point to it. Again you are modeling how to point to share an experience using a point gesture. Another example, you are at the park, see a kite and turn to your child to point it out with an excited "look, kite!" If your child does not turn and follow the direction of your point gently assist him by orienting his body and his face. You may be doing this already. But now you will recognize the importance of the social interaction and be vigilant to capitalize on very opportunity. You are laying a foundation for your child to share his or her experiences with you.

Help Your Child to Point

The next step is to teach your child to point purely to share his interests with you. The way to achieve this is to **follow his interests**. Again, not a new theme, we build on it over and over again. Think about it, why would your child want to share his excitement or joy about something if he isn't interested in it? Wait until he is excited about something then take his hand and fully prompt him to point to the item of interest. For example William is playing with his train. Out of curiosity he pushes a button and the train makes a loud whistle. He is thrilled! He turns to you and gives you a wonderful shared look. At that moment, when your heart skips a beat, keep your head cool and remember what you need to do next. Show big surprise (share his emotion with him), get down on the floor next to him, and point to the train. Wait to see if he imitates you and points on his own. If he does, immediately acknowledge and label the train. You could exclaim "yes, train!" or "choo choo!" or communicate that the whistle was unexpected by an exaggerated look of surprise or by saying "uh oh!" or some other expression of surprise. If he doesn't point take his hand, shape it into a point and fully prompt him to point to the train. Once again you are going to use errorless learning. If you need a reminder of what this is, go back to chapter 4. Refresh your memory on how to use a full physical prompt, decrease to a partial prompt, and then pull back further until you aren't prompting at all and your child completes the skill independently.

Often **sharing is about novelty**. We want to share new ideas with each other. We enjoy sharing new experiences with other people. Things that are novel will be your ally in finding moments when you can prompt a joint attention point. Here is an example of how you can set up a scenario that will give you several opportunities to prompt pointing. It is somewhat contrived, but rich in teaching opportunities. Find a bag that your child cannot see through. Choose a few small items that you know your child likes (juice box, cookie, toy car, picture book, and a few animals etc.). When your child is not present put all of the items in the bag and close it such that your child cannot see them. Then call him over and while holding the top mostly closed let him put his hand into the bag and feel around, not knowing what he is going to find. When his hand emerges with one of the items (horse), put on your animated face and ask excitedly "what is it?" Immediately take his other hand and prompt him to point to the horse. As he does, exclaim "horse!" and from there you can let the interaction flow naturally. If he wants to hold onto the horse and doesn't show immediate interest in finding out what else is in the bag, give him time. Let the pace feel natural. When you see the next opportunity arise (when he loses interest in the horse) call him over and enthusiastically show him the bag again. When he pulls out the next item immediately prompt him to point to it and enthusiastically share in the novelty with your excited affect and by naming the item. Most children think this game is fun. It has novelty, and they are motivated to look in the bag because it contains items of interest. Also, it is simple, you can keep it structured, and they know what to expect from the routine.

As you will see this game is very conducive to teaching a child how to point purely to share his enjoyment with you. In the beginning most children are unsure what it is all about, so it is up to you to familiarize them with the game, prompt the point completely if necessary, and remain animated even if they don't understand at first. After practicing the routine several times your child will show an emerging understanding of what he should do. You'll see the anticipation in his little body and face as he looks forward to what he may find in the bag. He'll need less prompting to point, he will show much more obvious enjoyment with you, and it will feel more and more natural. Remember though, your goal is to provide as much support as he needs to begin with, then slowly decrease your prompts until he is consistently pointing independently.

Require Eye-Contact

When your child is pointing independently purely to share his interests with you, he is ready for the next goal. Now we are going to work on the quality of his pointing gesture. Remember **children on the autism spectrum have difficulty coordinating various aspects of their communication**. As we did in chapter 4 when we talked about using a point to request, we are now going to expect that your child looks at you when he points as this significantly increases the quality of communication. Use the same strategies we discussed in chapter 4 to prompt his point (use as much prompting as is necessary at first then slowly decrease your prompt), the only difference this time is the purpose of the point. In chapter 4 the point was used to request, now the point is being used to share interest.

Showing

Showing is another important gesture in communication development and typically developing children show objects as early as 10 months. It is easier to teach children on the autism spectrum to point before teaching them to show objects. One reason is because when we teach pointing we start with using a point to request which is easier than teaching pointing for social reasons. Once children are pointing to request for food etc., they are then ready to point for social interaction. Thereafter they are ready to show.

By now you should be feeling comfortable creating opportunities to teach your child to point - to request items, to engage in joint attention, and using a prompt hierarchy to develop a gesture from full physical prompts to no prompts. The good news is that we are going to use exactly the same strategies to teach your child to show items. There is not much new for you to learn, except that the gesture changes. If you have successfully taught your child to point, this next part will be easy for you to teach.

Model and Prompt Showing

What does showing look like? A show is when a child extends their hand towards you and holds up an object for you to see. They do not release the object because their intention is not to give it you. Rather, their intention is to hold up something for you to see so that you can share their interest about that object. Just as we did with pointing you will teach showing by first modeling how to show and then by prompting your child to show to you.

Here is an example that is a variation of the bag game. Your child is sitting in a bubble bath but prior to getting in you and he selected some plastic toys that were thrown into the tub. The fun part is that the bubbles are now hiding everything. You fish around underneath and pull out a dinosaur! Right away you hold it up excitedly for your child to see and show him the dinosaur. Then it's his turn. Help as much (or as little) as he needs to feel around the bottom of the tub and find something to pull out. The moment his hand comes to the surface, take his hand and fully prompt him to show you. Then, just as you did with pointing, immediately label whatever he has in his hand with a very fun, animated voice and expression (as if this is your favorite game). The game can go on for quite a while and offer plenty of opportunity for practice as you both find hidden items. Again, it builds in novelty, things of interest to your child, and gives you multiple opportunities to teach showing and language. Also, your child is in the tub which is a wonderful place to have him captive (in a good sense of course). You see how this is something you can make part of an everyday activity like taking a bath. Now you are much more knowledgeable in how to use a bath time activity as a fun, but very powerful, teaching opportunity.

Require Eye-Contact

The next step should not come as a surprise; add eye-contact. Just as you did for pointing, set your child up to make eye-contact with you (if he isn't already) as he shows you his toy. If he does not make eye-contact gently guide his face to yours (as described in chapter 4 and earlier in this chapter).

The Importance of Your Face

Throughout this chapter and the previous one I have asked you repeatedly to use exaggerated affect with your child, to be highly animated in your facial expressions, to show a lot of excitement and enthusiasm, to overdo it. One reason is because it fits with what we are teaching. When we are very interested in something, we naturally become more animated and excited. Children also demonstrate this, even a one year old. When they bring you into their world, with one of those precious shared looks, very often it is with a beautiful smile. As they share their discovery with you, you can see it all over their face. They invite you in for you to do the same - to share your world with pleasure and awe.

We want the same for little ones on the autism spectrum. I am repeatedly struck by their seriousness, spending most of their days with a very neutral expression on their faces. One of my goals is to change that. When your child opens up, be it with a shared look, a point, or a show, you want to see the joy and the wonder in their face. However we can't prompt that. What I have seen over the many years of treating young children on the autism spectrum is that **the more animated we are with the children, the more likely they are to emulate our affect and begin to show it too**. After a while we see them open up, lighten their expressions, begin to smile, and begin to use joint attention with lovely expressions of joy. It's amazing to see and I celebrate every time. But it takes exaggeration on your part to make it happen. Just like everything else it will not happen overnight - instead it will take time to emerge. Also, just like everything else, no child is alike, they all respond in different ways and in their own time. Be patient and have fun with it.

KEY POINTS

- Joint attention is one of the earliest predictors of language.
- Shared looks, pointing, and showing are skills you can teach your child.

Shared Looks

- Use face-to-face interactions.
- Develop routines.
- Create a sense of anticipation.
- Exaggerate your affect.
- Surprise your child, change the routine.

Pointing

- Use novel experiences.
- First model how to use a point to share attention.
- Prompt your child to look in the direction of your point.
- Then prompt your child to point to things of interest.
- Use a prompt hierarchy to decrease prompts until your child points independently.
- Be enthusiastic when your child spontaneously points to share interest.
- Require eye-contact with the point.

Showing

- Use novel experiences.
- First model how to show something interesting.
- Prompt your child to look at what you are showing.
- Then prompt your child to show items of interest.
- Use a prompt hierarchy to decrease prompts until your child shows independently.
- Be highly responsive when your child spontaneously shows you items to share interest.
- Require eye-contact with the show.

PERSONAL NOTES

7 IMITATION

We have focused on two areas of difficulty for children on the autism spectrum: communication in chapters 3 and 4 where I explained how to increase your child's understanding of language and how to develop your child's functional communication; and social development in chapters 5 and 6 where I covered how you can change your child's social interactions through interactive baby games and shared attention. In this chapter I want to continue with social development and discuss imitation.

The ability to imitate another person's actions is another critical piece of our social development. We seldom consciously think about when we imitate other people yet it occurs naturally in many facets of our everyday lives. If we don't know which line to use at the bank we look at the people around us and follow them. In school, if children miss what the teacher said they look at the child next to them and do the same. When preschoolers sit in circle-time and sing songs with actions they watch the teacher and imitate her actions. If children are playing pretend they imitate each other. In a game such as "You be the daddy bear, I'll be the baby bear," one child growls like a bear, so does the other. One walks on all fours. The other does the same. We also use imitation to problem solve. We use it to participate in games and leisure activities. We use imitation to learn and it is a critical pre-requisite for learning language.

TYPICAL CHILDREN

Children begin to imitate actions in their first two years. As we discussed in chapter 5, infants imitate routine actions in face to face games like peek-a-boo as young as 10 months old. By 2 years of age, children imitate simple one step actions (clap hands, stomp feet, arms up, open mouth, smiling) and by 3 years they imitate two and three step action sequences. Typically developing children tend to be consistent in their imitation. After imitating an action once they reliably imitate it thereafter. Further typical children naturally imitate both adults and peers.

CHILDREN ON THE AUTISM SPECTRUM

Imitation does not develop naturally in children on the autism spectrum. Similar to other areas we have covered so far, we need to give them a targeted boost by teaching them specifically how to imitate us. When we begin teaching imitation, **children with autism benefit from a targeted, goal oriented approach with intense systematic guidance**. As your child imitates you more, you will be able to gradually change your teaching approach until he or she learns to imitate others spontaneously.

How do we begin? Many young children learn to imitate using elements of **discrete trial training**. We also used elements of this method in chapter 4. It is a widely accepted method of teaching children on the autism spectrum. This chapter will provide you with step by step instructions on how to teach imitation using discrete trial training. Similar to previous chapters, we are going to teach one skill at a time. This time though, we are going to be more systematic in our teaching approach.

The strategies that follow guide you how to teach your child to imitate one action, then a second, a third, and so on. You will learn: the power of reward; that practice is necessary for mastery; how to prompt effectively; the importance of generalization; and how to successfully introduce differentiation.

We begin with how to set you and your child up for success. That is, deciding where your teaching will be most effective and what to teach first which will involve some thought and planning.

STRATEGIES FOR CHANGE

Plan for Success

You will begin by teaching only one easy imitation action. You are going to teach it in a structured environment so that you can control the teaching and can implement the approach with maximum ease. Ideally you should be facing your child and have good physical control of her. You will direct the interaction which means you need to be within 1 foot of your child. There should be no distractions (toys, pets, etc.) within reach, and you should be able to control your child's actions. Possible physical settings include a high chair, bath tub, stroller or have your child facing you while seated in someone else's lap. When teaching imitation (and prompting your child) using discrete trial training, the physical setting plays an important role in your success.

After you have determined which setting may work, the next step is to identify the first imitation action that you will teach. Here are several guidelines to keep in mind:

1. Choose an easy action with one step. For example, tapping the tabletop once with the dominant hand. If your child is right handed, choose her right hand.

2. Think of a simple toy that your child does not already use that would incorporate a one step action. The toy itself does not have to be unusual or completely new to your child. However, you should choose something that will provide a new functional action for your child to learn. The action should be obvious to the toy (pushing a car, banging a drum). For example, if your child likes music, perhaps you could target hitting the key of a xylophone. Or if your child enjoys lights, consider putting one ring on a ringstack that lights up. If your child likes taking a bath, perhaps a simple bath toy would work. For example, squeezing a plastic duck until it quacks. Note that these examples take your child's interests into account or have some kind of fun consequence (the duck

quacks, the ringstack lights up). If your child is motivated, she will be more open to learning.

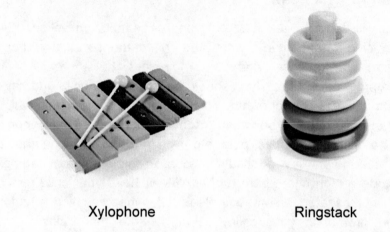

Xylophone   Ringstack

3. Try to think of an action where your child only uses one hand. The reason for this is that coordinating two hands can be difficult (even if we don't think so). Also some children on the autism spectrum have difficulty with bilateral coordination (coordinating the left and right sides of their body). It may not be obvious to you and possibly may not apply to your child. Regardless, it is an area that should not be cause for concern. It can be assessed by an occupational therapist and can be easily treated should the need arise. I mention it here only to make you think about which actions are suitable for your child. My goal is to set your child up for maximum success before you even begin so that once you demonstrate the action you want her to imitate, there is nothing that will prevent your child from imitating you (such as an action that is too difficult to physically manage).

When we teach imitation, the goal is for your child to do exactly what you do. In this context our objective is not to teach language, so we will keep our language very simple. The verbal instruction you will give your child for every action you teach is "do this". This way you are not overloading your child with multiple diverse stimuli (process different verbal instructions and imitate new physical actions). For each new physical imitation action you teach the verbal instruction will remain the same, the physical action will be different. However, we will carefully teach one action at a time, and slowly build up to a variety of actions.

Teach the First Action

Now that you have your first imitation action in mind, let me explain to you how you are going to instruct your child. Take the example of hitting a xylophone. If you say to your child "do this", then pick up the stick and hit the xylophone once, your child may not have any idea what you expect of her. Therefore when you teach a new action you need to give your child as much help as she needs to imitate the action you demonstrate. Sitting directly opposite your child, say "do this" and hit the xylophone once. Immediately after you finish your action, put the stick on the table and put your hand over hers so that she picks up the stick with your help and completely help her hand over hand to tap the xylophone. You should give your child as much help as she needs to successfully imitate your action. After you have finished, immediately praise your child with high affect. Be excited about her accomplishment even though you helped her. You have now completed what we call one discrete trial. **A discrete trial begins with your instruction, includes your prompt, your child's response, and then ends with your praise.**

The Power of Reward

Use simple language when you praise, one or two words at most. Examples are "Hooray!" or "Yes!" or "So good!" Along with your language give your child something that she will love. You can tickle her or give her a hug. You can massage her head; give her a favorite toy, or even a tiny piece of a favorite food like a cookie or cracker. However it is important that she really loves whatever you give her. **Your child should be looking for more, motivated and ready to interact with you**. Your praise must be motivating, or what we call "reinforcing" for your teaching to be effective. She is not going to immediately realize that your praise is directly linked with her performance. However you will be providing repeated opportunities for her to practice and receive praise. Over time she will make the link, when I do "x", mom gives me "y". When you achieve this, celebrate! It is powerful for learning.

Practice to Mastery

Many **children on the autism spectrum learn faster with a lot of repetition**. This means that you are going to practice the same trial we just described, exactly the same way over and over again. Your praise is the only component that should change in each trial. Would you want to hear "Hooray!" ten times? The key idea is not to become boring. You need to change your language and your reinforcement as much as is needed to keep your child motivated to work with you. Be creative, try different things. Think out of the box. Be silly, children love it. Be ridiculous, over the top, goofy. You don't have to act the clown, but you will maximize your child's response if you can make these times fun and enjoyable.

How to Prompt

You may be asking at this point, how on earth will my child learn and begin to imitate actions on his own if I am helping her to do the same action over and over again? Here is how the teaching develops. Once you have practiced the first action about 10 times (tapping the xylophone once) each time giving your child as much help as she needs, then try giving your child a little less help. See if she starts a portion of the action, or finishes the action, or initiates at any point during the action. Look for any hint that you can provide a little less help. If not, practice another 10 trials providing as much help as is needed. If your child does imitate part of the action, assess if you can do another 10 trials giving your child a little less help. How you decrease your prompting depends on your child.

Here are some examples on how you can reduce your prompts:

1. If you demonstrate tapping the xylophone and say "do this, and your child puts her hand on the stick, pause a second to see if she will initiate the remainder of the action. If not, put your hand over hers and help her to pick up the stick and tap the xylophone. For the next 10 trials always pause to let her put her hand on the stick independently, and then immediately help her to do the rest. Remember to praise her enthusiastically after each trial.

2. If she picks up the stick but does not tap, then put your hand over hers and help her to tap once. For the next 10 trials after you say "do this", pause and let her pick up the stick independently, then immediately help her to tap. Praise her enthusiastically, even though you helped her to complete the tap.

3. If she does the entire action by herself (picks up the stick and taps the xylophone once), but she does it very lightly, it doesn't matter, she does not need to be perfect. All you want her to do is understand the concept of imitation. Accept her effort and throw a party for her. Not literally of course, I mean really let her know that you think she is wonderful! However, just because she successfully completed the action once, it does not mean her imitation ability for the action is solid. Practice more of the same trials pausing right after you say "do this" and letting her complete the action on her own. If she independently imitates the action each time continue enthusiastically reinforcing her. If she shows some inconsistency help her to complete the full action as much and whenever is required.

The thinking behind this teaching approach is that at first your child probably doesn't know what you want from her. As a result, you provide as much help as she needs. Then little by little **reduce your prompts until your child can imitate the action independently** by herself. This can take many, many trials to achieve independence. How long? Children learn at different rates. One child may take 30 trials; another child may take one week practicing 20 trials each day. However if your child hasn't made much progress on the first action after two weeks, choose a different action (an even easier one) and start again. Don't despair if you do need to re-evaluate. It is not uncommon. In the clinic we monitor the children all the time. If a child does not progress on a goal, we evaluate why the child is having difficulty, and then make a change. It is a much better strategy than sticking to the same goal for an overly long period of time. Your next question: Why do some children not progress? Perhaps the action is too difficult. Maybe it requires more coordination or attention than your child can manage. Possibly it requires coordinating attention between multiple stimuli (looking at both you and the stick). In this case, an easier action may be just tapping the table once with an open hand.

Ensure Generalization

Once your child is imitating the first action completely on her own without any help from you, the next step is to make sure she can imitate the same action in different environments, and then with different people. Therefore if you practiced it in her high chair in the kitchen to begin with, now test if she can do it in her stroller in the kitchen and in the living room. Then instruct someone else on what to do and see if your child can imitate the action with a second person. Be prepared that your child may not complete the action as independently as she did when you practiced it in the first environment. Simply choose a second environment and practice it there just as you did initially, giving your child as much help as she needs. When she is independently imitating your action, choose a third environment and practice it there. Then ask someone else to practice it with her. What we are doing is making sure that your child's learning is truly solid and flexible. What I mean by flexible is that she shows her newly learned skill in different environments, and with different people. This is what we call **generalization, the ability to transfer a new concept or skill from where and how it was initially learned to different contexts**. This results in flexible, useful learning as your child can use the skill in everyday opportunities. The reason it is important to make sure that your child is generalizing what she has learned is because some children on the autism spectrum learn concepts in a specific context and then do not use them elsewhere. This leads to extremely limited learning that is not useful for everyday development. For example if your child learns to wave bye-bye with you in the kitchen at home it does not necessarily mean that she will use it to communicate bye-bye to her grandparents at the front door when they leave after a visit. Be vigilant, never take generalization for granted.

Teach the Second Action

When your child has generalized the first imitation action (tap xylophone) and is successfully completing it without any help in about 8 out of 10 trials, then you are ready to teach the second action. Choose another very easy action, but make sure it is very different from the first one. If you used the xylophone for the first action do not choose another tapping action for the second one. Or if you chose putting a ring on a ring stack avoid choosing a second action that requires placing an item on a base. You should teach actions that are very distinct from each other so that your child does not become confused. Sometimes **children on the autism spectrum do not pay attention long enough at the outset to distinguish one action from another** if they are very similar.

If the second imitation action is placing a block in a box, get two blocks and one box. Say "do this" and put one block in the box. Wait a few seconds to see if your child imitates the action on her own with the second block. If not, help her as much as is needed to complete the action. Then just as before, praise her enthusiastically, no matter how much help you gave her. An important strategy to remember is that when you introduce a second action practice it separately from anything else. This means you should practice it on its own at a different time than the first action. You should definitely keep practicing the first action (not at the same intensity, just 5 or so trials every day to make sure that your child's newly learned skill remains solid). Since most children learn better in the morning, work on the new (second action) in the morning when your child is fresh. Then practice the first (mastered action) in the afternoon. That way you will keep both actions distinctly separate and decrease the possibility of your child becoming confused. Build your second action up to independence just as you did the first one. If at any point, your child becomes inconsistent in imitating any action, provide a little help again until your child is consistently independent. Then ensure that your child's learning generalizes to different locations, people and even a different block and different box.

Teach Differentiation

When your child is independently imitating both of the actions (action 1 – tap xylophone, action 2 – block in box), the next step is to practice them together. In the morning when your child is fresh for learning work on both actions together. Stick to exactly the same format. Say "do this" and show/model tapping on the xylophone. After your child responds correctly, praise her, and progress immediately to the next trial. Say "do this" and show/model putting a block in the box. Practice approximately 10 trials alternating the xylophone and block in box. If all looks good (independent actions by the child), then progress to generalization. Practice both actions one after the other in a variety of environments and with at least one other person. If either action is troublesome don't move on. Give your child whatever help is needed for the action with which she is having difficulty (as little help as possible, but enough to complete the action). Keep practicing both skills one after the other until both are consistent and generalized (your child is imitating both actions in different environments, with different people, and with a different box or blocks).

Teach the Third Action

Now you are ready to introduce the third imitation action. Again, choose an action that is very different from the first two. A good example is to place a ring on a ringstack. Just as you did before, work on this new action by itself in the morning. Then practice the other two mastered skills (action 1 – tap xylophone, action 2 – block in box) in the afternoon as you did in the previous step.

When the newest action (ringstack) is independent you are going to work on all three actions together (ringstack, xylophone, block in box) with the newest action (ringstack) alternating between the other two mastered actions (xylophone, block in box). I will guide you through this procedure as it can be confusing.

The ringstack is the newest skill, therefore it is the action we need to focus on the most. We are going to give your child extra opportunity to practice it to ensure that she can clearly discriminate between the new skill and the previously mastered skills. Therefore your child should imitate the ringstack action first. Then do any one of the previously mastered skills. In our example we will choose the xylophone (mastered action 1). Now go back to the ringstack (new action). Next, present another mastered skill. We will choose block in box (mastered action 2). Return to the ringstack (new action). It does not matter which mastered action you choose to present first. You could have chosen the xylophone or block in box. What matters is that you practice the new action alternating with one of the mastered actions (xylophone or block in box).

new action → mastered action 1   → **new action** → mastered action 2 → **new action** → mastered action 1 → **new action** → mastered action 2 etc.

For example:

ringstack (new action) → xylophone (action 1) → **ringstack (new action)** → block in box (action 2) → **ringstack (new action)** → xylophone (action 1) → **ringstack (new action)** → block in box (action 2) etc.

Or, as the following sequence shows, mastered action 2 can be selected after the new action.

new action → mastered action 2   → **new action** → mastered action 1 → **new action** → mastered action 2 → **new action** → mastered action 1 etc.

For example:

ringstack (new action) → block in box (action 2) → **ringstack (new action)** → xylophone (action 1) → **ringstack (new action)** → block in box (action 2) → **ringstack (new action)** → xylophone (action 1) etc.

If your child is successfully imitating all three actions, she is ready for the next challenge of practicing two mastered skills and then a new skill. Present the newest skill (in our example this is the ringstack) followed by each of the mastered skills (xylophone, and block in box). Again it does not matter which of the mastered skills you present first. What matters is that you present the newest action (ringstack) every third trial.

new action → mastered action 1 → mastered action 2 →
new action → mastered action 1 → mastered action 2 etc.

For example:

ringstack (new action) → xylophone (action 1) → block in box
(action 2) → **ringstack (new action)** → xylophone (action 1)
→ block in box (action 2) etc.

Or, as the following sequence shows, mastered action 2 can be
selected after the new action.

new action → mastered action 2 → mastered action 1 →
new action → mastered action 2 → mastered action 1 etc.

For example:

ringstack (new action) → block in box (action 2) → xylophone
(action 1) → **ringstack (new action)** → block in box (action 2)
→ xylophone (action 1) etc.

If your child does well with this, then you can progress to
practicing the three actions in any order. To consider them all as
mastered your child should be able to imitate any of them in
whatever order you present them. However, just as before, if she
begins to have difficulty with any of the actions take a step back
and prompt her (as little as needed, but enough to complete the
action) until the action is independent. After successfully
practicing all three in random order, also make sure all three are
generalized (your child is imitating them in different locations and
with several people). These three will now be considered your
mastered set. You will continue to review them in the afternoon
to ensure that your child maintains her learning. This will be
easier to accomplish as you will be able to practice them in
different places and with different people (grandparents, uncle,
aunt, babysitter, etc.).

Teach the Fourth Action

I will go through a couple more steps to make sure you are clear on the procedure. None of it is much different: new action; then repeat new action alternating it with previous mastered actions. For our fourth action we will select putting a car on a ramp and pushing it. It should be a short ramp to ensure that the action is brief (to keep the focus on imitation).

Car Ramp

You will practice the new action (putting a car on a ramp and pushing it) on its own in the morning giving your child as much help as is needed. When your child is imitating you without any help, then you are ready to introduce the car ramp action into the mastered set (action 1 - xylophone, action 2 - block in box, action 3 - ringstack).

Again you need to introduce the new action systematically into the mastered set. Start with action #4 (car ramp). Then present any one of the previously mastered actions (1, 2 or 3); we will choose xylophone (mastered action 1). Then go back to car ramp (new skill). Then present another mastered skill; we will choose block in box (mastered action 2). Return to car ramp (new skill). Next, ring stack (mastered action 3), followed by car ramp (new skill). Go back to xylophone (mastered action 1), then car ramp (new skill), and so on. As you did before present the newest action (car ramp) every alternate trial to give your child plenty of practice in differentiating it from the other three actions.

When this looks stable progress a little further. Now present the goal you are targeting (the newest action) with two mastered actions in between. It does not matter which two mastered actions you choose or what order you present them. Indeed now that we have more than 2 mastered actions in our mastered set (xylophone, block in box, ringstack), we can present any of them as long as we insert the new skill every third trial.

It should look like this:

new action → any mastered action → any different mastered action → **new action** → any mastered action → any different mastered action → **new action** etc.

Here is one possible example using our imitation actions:

car ramp (new action) → ringstack (action 3) → block in box (action 2) → **car ramp (new action)** → ringstack (action 3) → tap xylophone (action 1) → **car ramp (new action)** etc.

The thinking behind the method is to extend your child's memory a little longer and give her practice in remembering the newest skill. You can see how carefully we proceed. Little by little we extend the amount of time (number of mastered trials) she has to work before recalling a new skill. At this point, if all of the actions are consistently independent, you can progress to working on all four actions in any order. Lastly, don't forget generalization (different locations and with different people). When it makes sense, try to generalize with different toys as well. As I suggested earlier in the chapter, you could use a different box and different blocks to make sure your child can imitate the action with different items. You could use any type of box that you have at home, an empty shoe box is suitable. However most families will only have one ringstack or one xylophone and it would be unreasonable to acquire a second one. Therefore use common sense and only generalize to different items or toys when it is reasonable for you to do so.

When you target the fifth imitation action, you will do it exactly the same way as we just did for the last imitation action. Present it in isolation, then when it is mastered, alternate it with one mastered action, then target the new skill every third action. Please note that presenting two mastered actions in between the new skill is enough. No matter how large your mastered set becomes you only need to present two mastered actions before you present the new action again. Lastly, present them in random order. Then generalize.

You can keep adding new skills one at a time making sure that your child does not lose any mastered skills while learning new material.

Create a Solid Foundation

Aim to teach 20-30 separate imitation actions. It may sound like an enormous undertaking, but after your child has mastered the first few initial actions it is likely that his or her **rate of learning will speed up**. In other words, as you introduce new actions, you can progress much more quickly from prompting to independence. You may be wondering how soon you should expect to see this. Again, every child is different and they have different strengths. You may see your child's learning speed up after the fifth action, it may take ten actions, or even more. When this happens, obviously you should progress at a rate that matches your child's learning. Move your child forward as fast as his or her learning allows but be vigilant at all times to ensure that the mastered skills remain steady. If you see a pattern of incorrect responding, slow down and take some time to reconsolidate and strengthen. It will be more than worth your time. Your child's development will be more stable with a stronger foundation. This is critical for children on the autism spectrum. Do not panic if things appear to be moving slowly. Every child learns at a different pace. Take your time, remain methodical, work at the pace that your child needs and consider enlisting the help of other family members or even a babysitter to help you achieve your goal.

Why 20-30 actions? I find that at this point most children have a good grasp of introductory imitation. Usually by the time a child has learned about 30 actions with very systematic teaching, the way I explained it in this chapter, you will see her learning speed up. Then something exciting happens. **You should start to see what you wanted from the outset; your child will imitate new actions in everyday activities without any systematic teaching**.

Now that your child has mastered basic imitation she will be ready for more advanced **imitation which is not only an invaluable social skill, but one used in many aspects of learning and language development**. For example, she will need to be able to imitate two and even three actions in a sequence, oral movements and speech sounds, and complex actions from other children. The foundation you are building now is essential for your child's continued development.

KEY POINTS

- Imitation is an important part of early social development.

- It is an essential prerequisite for developing speech.

- Teach one action at a time to mastery:

    Present each new action in isolation.

    When the new action is mastered, alternate it with one previously mastered action.

    Then present the new skill every third action.

    Lastly, practice all mastered actions in random order.

    Then generalize.

- Carefully reduce your prompts.

- Reinforce success at every stage.

- Check that your child can differentiate between mastered actions before adding anything new.

- Make sure each new action is generalized (different people and different locations, different objects or toys only when they are readily available).

- Slow down, ensure a solid foundation.

PERSONAL NOTES

8 CHANGE UNUSUAL BEHAVIORS

This chapter covers another key area where you can make a significant difference in how your child interacts with his or her environment. Chapter 2 described the core characteristics of children on the autism spectrum. One of them is an unusual focus on specific aspects of the environment, on things that typical children do not focus on. I want to spend some time on this, to explain what I mean, what you should be looking for, when you should be concerned, and of course how to intervene for change.

Children on the autism spectrum exhibit unusual behaviors that relate to the five senses (seeing, smelling, hearing, touching and tasting). They tend to either avoid or seek one of these senses much more than their typical peers. This impacts learning because **whenever a child is either seeking unusual sensory stimulation or avoiding experiences they are not learning from their environment as they should be**. You may not realize it but children who are developing normally are learning from their environment in a meaningful way all the time. They rarely miss opportunities to learn from their natural environment. Neither should your child.

SENSORY SEEKERS

The sections below describe several modalities in which children on the autism spectrum seek sensory input (visual, tactile, auditory, smell and taste). Also discussed are several criteria that will help you determine whether your child's behavior is normal or not, and why children engage in these behaviors. Finally I present strategies within each sensory modality that you can use to change inappropriate behavior.

Visual Behaviors

Children can seek sensory stimulation in abnormal ways often resulting in one sensory modality predominating. What can these behaviors look like? Children who seek visual stimulation may change or distort their visual perception or scrutinize details. For example, a father of a child in my clinic reported that his child loved trains but instead of sitting on the rug to push them, he would lie down and put his cheek on the rug to watch the wheels turn. The child's father thought it was somewhat quirky but probably harmless. He was frustrated though, because he couldn't play meaningfully with his son. Every time the father attempted to get his son to sit up, barely a minute passed before his son was lying down again watching the wheels of the trains.

Another child spent hours on his bed watching the sun's rays through the horizontal window blinds. He was also fascinated with the shadows that the lights made on the ceiling and the repetitive movement of the ceiling fan above the bed. He could spend hours in his bedroom completely absorbed. Since he was their first child, the parents didn't know this behavior was unusual.

Another child turned his head at an angle to see the edges of things, like the continuous edge of the kitchen counter or the hem of a dress. He also held objects very close to his face. Instead of playing with toys, he mostly scrutinized them in front of his eyes. Many children on the autism spectrum who seek stimulation in the visual mode engage in these types of behaviors.

Keep two thoughts in mind as you consider whether your child demonstrates these types of behaviors. Children with autism engage in many different kinds of unusual behaviors. Second, autism is a spectrum. The underlying symptoms are the same, but they can manifest themselves in many different ways. Try not to be quick to discard the notion that your child does not fit what I just described. Keep reading to make sure. If this does turn out to be an area you need to pay attention to you need to be informed and know how to intervene.

Tactile Behaviors

While some children seek atypical visual experiences, others self-stimulate ("stim" is the shortened and frequently used term) in the tactile mode. For example two year old Sarah loved to rub things. She always wanted to stroke her mother's hair, she insisted on rubbing anything soft between her thumb and forefinger whenever she could, and she rubbed soft toys against her cheeks. The problem was that Sarah's tactile needs interfered with her participation and learning in everyday activities. For example, when Sarah stroked her mother's hair she paid almost no attention to anything else around her. She missed countless social and language opportunities. Further, because her toy bear was usually pressed against her cheek Sarah never pretended to put him to bed or feed him etc. Indeed any time Sarah encountered a soft material she disengaged from other activities to explore the sensation of the material.

Auditory Behaviors

Children who self-stimulate in the auditory mode often engage in repetitive speech or singing. One little boy hummed all day long. Another said the same few unintelligible sounds repeatedly regardless of the activity. He also banged anything that emitted sound (he repeatedly opened and slammed doors to hear the noise, he consistently banged his cup on the table). The way you can decide if an auditory behavior is unusual or not, is to ask yourself if it serves a purpose and if it is meaningful. Is your child using speech to communicate meaningfully? Is your child singing at appropriate times, or is it interfering with how he interacts with you or his world? **Self-stimulatory behaviors are a problem when they interfere with a child's normal functioning and**

development. If they are preventing how your child responds to his natural environment they are a problem.

Smell and Taste

Unusual olfactory (smell) and oral (licking) behaviors are less common than the other sensory modalities. Children who seek unusual olfactory experiences may smell everything they pick up. Often they seek stronger smells that typical children consider unpleasant. It is the frequency with which they smell things, and what they choose to smell that should alert you. Use the same criteria to evaluate behaviors associated with licking. For example a child might walk by a table and lick it, or lick the soil in a flowerbed. These behaviors are quite different than what one sees in typical children.

Normal Versus Abnormal?

The above examples are obvious but I know many parents will find it difficult to decide if their child's behavior is abnormal. Here are several key guiding principles that will help you. First think about the **frequency** of the behavior. It is unlikely that a typical child will engage in these kinds of behaviors, but if they do it will be rare or very occasional. Therefore pay attention if your child frequently engages in an unusual behavior. Second think about **intensity**. Does your child become engrossed in the behavior to the extent that he is not aware of anything else around him? Third think about the **amount of time** your child spends engaging in the behavior. Many children on the autism spectrum spend long periods of time engaged in these types of activities. For example, one adorable two-year old would spend hours at a stretch spinning any item that he could (toy plates, rings from the ring stacker). He visually fixated on the spinning object, his entire body tight with excitement and his hands flapping rapidly. Lastly, is it **difficult to stop your child** from engaging in the behavior? Some children resist a lot when they are prevented from stimming, or even tantrum when you try to change their activity. Other children may not necessarily protest, they just resume stimming within a few minutes, and you find yourself constantly preventing them from engaging in the behavior. Keep in mind though that your child's behavior need not meet all four criteria (frequency, intensity, duration, resistance) to be concerning. Just one of the criteria is enough for you to take action.

Reasons for Sensory Seeking Behaviors

Why do children on the autism spectrum engage in these unusual behaviors? Honestly, we don't really know. Professionals hypothesize that the underlying reason is related to how ordinary everyday sensory stimulation is processed. Essentially we are all constantly bombarded by a multitude of sensory input in the form of visual images, sounds, smells, etc. Much of the time we take it all for granted and barely notice the breeze on our face, the smell of flowers, or the feel of our sweater against our skin. Despite our minimal conscious awareness of all the sensations we encounter, our neurological system efficiently registers and processes it all.

It is thought that **children with autism process sensory information differently** than we do. Even though they are exposed to the same environment as typical children, some children with autism do not receive enough stimulation. The result is that their neurological system becomes dysregulated (out of balance). This can result in sensory seeking behaviors to compensate for the deficit. For some children it is visual, for others it is auditory, for others it is olfactory or oral. These types of behaviors are also observed in young children in overcrowded orphanages where they are held by a caregiver for at most one hour in a day. Essentially the children spend days in their cribs with minimal stimulation. These children do not have autism. However their sensory seeking behaviors are similar to children on the autism spectrum. They provide their own sensory input in an attempt to provide their neurological systems with essential stimulation.

STRATEGIES FOR CHANGE (SENSORY SEEKERS)

What do we do about it? Before you think about changing your child's behavior it is **critical that you first understand why the behavior is occurring** or what is driving the behavior. When you understand the reason for the behavior you can think about how to change it in an informed and effective way.

We begin with undesirable behaviors that are driven by a need to obtain sensory input. Your first reaction may be to question if there is any way to change them. You may be thinking that it will be impossible to change a behavior that is caused by a need in your child's neurological system. The good news is that **you can change unusual sensory behaviors** if you are observant, strategic and persistent. We all seek sensory input in a variety of ways even though we are constantly exposed to sensory experiences. Think of how good a massage or a swim feels, we buy perfume because we like the smell, music is a part of our everyday lives, and many love the taste of chocolate. These are just a few of the experiences that we seek because we enjoy the sensations that they offer. The difference is that we enjoy socially acceptable sensory experiences, stimulation that society considers normal. That is key in how you are going to change your child's behavior. In simple terms you will prevent your child every time he seeks sensory stimulation in an atypical way. Instead you will provide your child with frequent opportunities to obtain the stimulation he is seeking in acceptable ways. That is the crux of how you will change your child's behavior. Of course I will provide you with more details of how to implement these seemingly simple techniques. First I will give you examples of how you can provide appropriate ways for your child to get the input he needs. Then I will discuss how to redirect your child every time he seeks inappropriate stimulation.

Visual Seekers

Give your child toys that are visually interesting as a way to provide appropriate visual input. Car ramps are a winner. The boys love them as they can watch their car speed all the way down the ramp. It is even more visually stimulating if the ramp has curves. Other appropriate means are toys that light up, pop up toys, and toys with parts that move (e.g. a bead maze). Bubbles are wonderful, they are visually very interesting as they expand from the bubble wand, as they float through the air and as they pop. You can also make it a social experience by sharing in the excitement of blowing bubbles, racing cars, etc.

Bead Maze

Tactile Seekers

Think carefully about the type of tactile experience your child seeks. Some children seek deep pressure. These children often purposely crash into things, may dive headlong into the sand box, and constantly seek ways for their body to receive major impact from other surfaces and people. As a more appropriate alternative, try massages; squeeze their arms from the shoulders down to the wrist; encourage jumping on a trampoline, get them to push their chair to the table (the pushing provides deep joint compression); have them wear a backpack with a few books in it (the weight provides input); give them a firm play-doh or child putty as it requires some work to pull it apart. Every time you touch a child like this, try to be mindful that he prefers more pressure. Even when you are caressing your child, make it firmer. Other children prefer light touch; they respond well to tickles on their arms, legs and back, you can rustle their hair, or with supervision, let them sift their hands through a bowl of raw rice or beans.

Other children seek squishy textures. They want their hands in the pudding, can spend hours playing in the mud, or may enjoy the feel of paint or glue on their hands. These children usually love rubber squishy balls. Offer them lotion on their hands a few times a day, give them play-doh, place shaving cream onto a tray and let them make shapes and swirls, you can add food coloring to make it more interesting. You can do the same thing with corn starch (just add a little water); it provides a firmer consistency than shaving cream does. Let them join you in the kitchen when you are making chocolate pudding, cookies, a cake, etc., anything that has a good squishy feel.

Auditory Seekers

Give your child toys that make sounds as a more appropriate way to get sensory input. We have a toy in the clinic that makes a unique noise every time a shape is placed in the correct slot. It is particularly effective in providing good auditory stimulation because it is tall and elongated; the noise continues the entire time it takes the shape to fall from the top to the bottom. Children love it. Musical instruments are effective, indeed music in general works well. If your child tolerates headphones you can give him extra stimulation without having to listen to it yourself (but make sure the volume is low).

Oral or Olfactory Seekers

It is important to bear in mind that all typically developing infants mouth objects in the first 18 months and particularly when they are teething. This is their way of learning about their world. Before you think about whether to intervene on your child's oral behavior first consider if your child might be developmentally at the age where mouthing is appropriate. By this I mean that even if your child is 3 years old, for example, it could be that the skills he is demonstrating in many areas of development are more like those of a younger child. If this is the case, then it is not necessary for you to intervene; you can consider it a normal stage of your child's development. Use any book with normal developmental milestones to determine what milestones your child has reached and where he is developmentally compared to typical development.

On the other hand many children on the autism spectrum seek unusual oral input. Many seek chewy textures; they seem to crave experiences that will provide pressure in and around their mouths. As a more appropriate alternative, you can give your child foods that naturally provide resistance and require extended chewing. Bagels are an easy choice, also dried fruits and any kind of cured meats. Most young children swallow gum, for that reason I would not recommend you try it. You can also give your child a teether; there are many available with a wide variety of textures and shapes. If your child licks just about everything he picks up before he puts it in his mouth, I would suggest giving him a few licks of a lollipop (or anything else that is appropriate) at frequent intervals throughout the day. The same idea applies to children who seek olfactory experiences. First determine what type of smells your child seeks and then provide your child with a similar but appropriate smell experience at regular intervals throughout the day.

Replace Inappropriate Activities

The section above gave you activities that can replace your child's inappropriate sensory seeking with more appropriate activities that will serve the same sensory needs. Decide which sensory modality your child uses to provide himself with self-stimulatory experiences. Observe him closely to further "refine your understanding of the behavior (you may know the behavior is tactile, but specify the type of tactile experience, e.g. light, deep, squishy). Then think about the many different ways that you can provide similar acceptable experiences that are manageable for you and your family. Recognize that your child needs frequent stimulation. Therefore be proactive and provide your child with opportunities to obtain what he is seeking at regular intervals throughout the day. By offering frequent opportunities for appropriate stimulation children on the autism spectrum are less likely to seek out inappropriate activities.

Redirect Inappropriate Behaviors

Your next goal will be to immediately stop your child every time he seeks inappropriate input. You can achieve this in different ways. One way is to simply redirect your child every time he engages in inappropriate sensory seeking behaviors without actually saying "no." Rather simply draw his attention to something else and if necessary physically prompt him to stop. For example, if your child seeks visual input by staring at fans, light coming through blinds, flickering lights, etc., every time he stares at them such that he does not pay attention to other things around him, simply block his gaze by holding your hand briefly in front of his face or eyes, and then draw his attention to something else. You can pull out a book for him to look at, blow bubbles, direct him to play with the cars and ramp or if you are outside, point out a flower, an airplane or a passing car.

Another approach is to give your child clear feedback that what he is doing is unacceptable. In the clinic we use "uh oh" instead of "no." The children tend to respond well to the alternative reprimand as it conveys a message that what the child is doing is unacceptable but the negative tone is softer than "no!" Use the same example above and apply the "uh oh" to it. With this approach each time your child becomes visually fixated give him the direct feedback that what he is doing is not okay, "uh oh." Use a neutral tone of voice, it is not meant to be punishment, just feedback. Of course you can also both block his gaze and provide a verbal "uh oh" at the same time.

Other Sensory Behaviors

In this section we will discuss behaviors that are self-stimulatory but the purpose of the sensory behavior is not clear. Hand flapping is a good example. If your child hand flaps you may be wondering how it fits into one of the categories I mentioned above. It does not serve as visual stimulation (most children on the autism spectrum who flap, usually flap with their hands out to the side and they do not look at them), nor does it provide olfactory, tactile or auditory feedback. However if you carefully observe your child, you will soon realize that he flaps when stimulated by one of the sensory seeking experiences we have discussed. Remember the little boy who would spin items for hours. He was stimming in the visual mode, but as he did his whole body became tense with excitement, and he flapped his arms continuously. Think of hand and/or arm flapping as an energy release. He was unaware that he was flapping. His exclusive focus was the visual experience of watching items spin.

How should you intervene? Use the same basic idea that we discussed in the section above. Find an alternative means for him to release his energy. First remove all obvious items that can be spun. Then provide him with alternative appropriate ways to obtain the visual input he is seeking. One of the toys he loved had a lever he could pull which made a dial spin; when the dial landed on a specific animal it made the corresponding animal sound. He also loved bubbles. However, because these toys are visually stimulating, essentially serving the same purpose for him as the inappropriate spinning did, it should not be surprising that he flapped whenever he engaged with them. Again you can approach this in different ways. You can choose not to draw his attention to the flapping, and simply place his hands down every time he flaps. Some children learn to inhibit the flapping when you repeatedly prevent the behavior. However the problem with only redirecting his hands is that although you have provided an appropriate alternate medium for him to get visual stimulation, you have not given a different way to release the energy (excitement). Therefore another way to intervene is to take his hands every time he flaps, put them together and physically prompt him so that he is squeezing his hands together. The squeezing provides a wonderful physical release. It works well because a child can easily squeeze his hands together no matter where he is, it looks more acceptable than flapping, and it provides a way for your child to be able to release that excited energy independent of anyone or anything. You may not like this intervention for one reason or another. Regardless, I want you to understand the reasoning behind the intervention. That way you can come up with something else (e.g. squeeze a small, soft ball) that will be both acceptable to you (and to other children and adults in his environment) and effective at changing your child's behavior.

SUMMARY: SENSORY SEEKERS

First evaluate which sensory need is driving your child's inappropriate behavior. Then **think about activities that will provide your child with alternate appropriate sensory input that will serve the same function as his inappropriate behaviors**. The key to this approach is for you to be proactive, not reactive. That is, you need to take the initiative and make sure your child receives appropriate sensory input frequently throughout the day. Then stop and redirect your child every time he engages in inappropriate sensory seeking behaviors.

SENSORY AVOIDERS

Some of you will be shaking your head because there are also **children on the autism spectrum who avoid sensory experiences rather than seek them out**. These children are sensory avoidant; they become distressed when they come into contact with certain sensory experiences. They will do whatever they can to avoid the experience. Many children cannot tolerate a variety of wet substances that stick to their hands such as paint, shaving cream, or glue. Others have difficulty tolerating certain foods because of the texture, the smell, or the taste. Some children are irritated by the tags on their clothes; often these children are comfortable only in certain types of clothing materials. Others become very distressed with loud noise, or certain types of sounds (most common are sounds made by a vacuum cleaner, hairdryer, blender, etc.). There are children that will not walk barefoot on sand or grass. Every child is different, what may be very distressing for one child, may be unremarkable for another.

In the section below I describe how to use gradual desensitization, an effective strategy for changing overly avoidant behavior.

STRATEGIES FOR CHANGE (SENSORY AVOIDERS)

Gradual Desensitization

The idea is to **slowly expose your child to whatever sensory experience he is avoiding and help him to tolerate it**. Begin by having him tolerate just a small amount. Choose a time when you can focus exclusively on your child so that you can be available to help him through his distress. For example, if your child avoids touching textures like wet paint, begin by having him put the tip of his finger in the paint for a second (you may need to take his finger and prompt him to touch it). Then immediately let him wash it off. Even if he is crying and generally distressed, give him a lot of praise for touching it. As he becomes more used to it, slowly you will expect more from him, perhaps to tolerate having paint on more than just a fingertip, and then for longer periods of time. Essentially you are **gradually desensitizing** your child.

There are several strategies you can use to make it easier. One strategy is to make sure your child feels comfortable in the environment before you push him to touch the paint. You could have his favorite music playing in the background. It may help him calm after the unpleasant experience. Another strategy is to count out loud. As you dip his fingertip into the paint, count "1, 2, 3, all done". After several days your child will have more predictability as to how long he has to hold out (even as you count for longer). Counting is a good initial strategy, but as your child tolerates more, try to decrease and then eliminate the counting so that the activity becomes more normal.

Here is another example of how you can approach sensory avoidance. We will use the same strategy of slowly desensitizing your child, but this time we will use the sound of a carpet vacuum cleaner as the intolerable stimulus. Depending on how sensitive your child is to the noise will determine how far away from the actual vacuum cleaner you will start. Some children become very distressed several rooms away. If that is the case, begin there, literally a few rooms away from where the vacuum cleaner is located. From the moment you turn the vacuum on help your child to cope with the sound by covering his ears (just as we would when a siren blasts our ears). You can begin with having the vacuum on for several seconds if you think that is as much as your child can manage. The moment the vacuum is turned off, remember to reward him (see chapter 7 on how to reward your child), even if you had to help him cope and even if he was distressed. If necessary spend some time helping him to calm, and then redirect his attention to something else so that the experience is behind him. Every few days expect him to tolerate the noise for a little longer. You should see his distress decrease as he realizes that he can cover his ears and that he can cope, even though the sound is unpleasant. Just as we are empowered when we feel successful, children experience the same sense of mastery. The more you can reward him for tolerating unpleasant experiences with less distress, the more motivated he will be to overcome his avoidant behaviors. On days when he needs less help to cope make your reward and praise even stronger. Once he is tolerating the sound for longer periods of time (there is no magic number but a minute at least is reasonable), you can start to move him closer to the vacuum cleaner. Again you will do this gradually. It is also important that you work on one goal at a time. Therefore as you decrease the distance between him and the vacuum, don't expect him to tolerate the sound for longer periods of time. If he was coping for one minute, the next step will be for him to tolerate the sound for one minute but closer to the actual source of the sound.

Sensory avoidance in the domain of food and eating is an area that can be more difficult to change. Many children on the autism spectrum eat a limited range of foods; often sensory avoidance plays a large part in their resistance. For children who have aversions to certain textures, tastes, or smells, tolerance develops very gradually. Professional guidance may be needed for this as it is not straightforward. Knowing what types of foods to introduce first and how to progress can be an art. In the clinic we often use a desensitization approach to increase food tolerance with similar elements to what I described above in the paint and vacuum cleaner examples. We begin by insisting that the child keep a small piece of the aversive food on his plate alongside a preferred food. When this is achieved, in addition to keeping the food on his plate, he is expected to briefly touch it (we prompt as much as necessary to achieve the goal). When he can independently touch the food without distress he is expected to bring the food up to his mouth and kiss it. Following that, the expectation is that he puts it in his mouth and keeps it there briefly, and then he can spit it out. The last step is for the child to swallow the food. It is vital for children to receive a lot of encouragement and praise throughout each step as they work to overcome their resistance. Also, we view parents as key partners in their child's treatment, and a decision to intervene in areas like those described in this chapter always occur with parent consent and collaboration.

I understand it may be difficult for you to see your child in distress. Some children can have strong reactions when they encounter an intolerable sensory experience. My goal though is to encourage and empower you to find the determination to achieve change. I have seen over and over again how much children can change if we push them. Many preschoolers who arrive in our clinic will not put their finger anywhere near textures like paint, glue, and shaving cream. They refuse to participate in any activity that requires them to get their fingers a little wet. This does not bode well for preschool where children participate in art projects every day, and where touching a variety of media and textures is considered routine as is regular hand washing. Therefore in the clinic we start intervening slowly just as I described. Each day we help each child tolerate a little more. By the end of their stay with us (an average of 10 weeks) many two year olds are independently putting their whole hand into the paint and happily finger painting. Parents are in disbelief at how much progress their child made given how distressed they were at the outset. That is the beauty of working with young children. Often what seems impossible is not if you push them a little, and give them a lot of love at the same time. The key though is for you to remain persistent and resilient. You have to be calm and strong, you have to be the support for your child to help him or her change. Believe that change will occur even if it is gradual.

Even if you have the best of intentions it may be difficult for you to follow through and effectively intervene. Only you know what you can manage and what is too much for you. If you really feel you are not emotionally ready, ask someone else to intervene. Some parents feel that they have to be responsible for everything and involved without question. If you feel that way, think about whether you are holding your child back. By letting someone else help you, you may be helping your child more.

FLEXIBILITY IS KEY

In this last section I want to bring your attention to flexibility. In the context of children with autism spectrum disorders **flexibility encompasses being able to adapt to change** as the situation demands. It involves the ability to cope with unexpected situations even if they are not what we would like. The more adaptable we are, the better we are at surviving. Think about this on a large scale (life in general), or on a much smaller scale (how we handle all the unexpected everyday events). The more flexible we are the more we can enjoy life and not be upset about something unexpected that occurs.

Children on the autism spectrum often react to changes in their environment with an inflexibility that is beyond what is considered normal. It is another aspect of how their responses to the environment can be very different than that of a typical child. I mentioned this briefly in the first chapter; it is one of three main areas that we evaluate when considering whether a child may have an autism spectrum disorder.

It is not uncommon for parents to report that they have to take the same route home each day to prevent their child from tantruming the whole way home. Another example is Tim, a three year old we had in our clinic who would not wear his long sleeves rolled or pushed up. This was a problem any time he was involved in a messy activity like painting or playing at a water table. His sleeves became completely wet and then he wanted to change his shirt. Another example is Sammy who insisted on carrying a video from home to the clinic each day. Two year old Brian would only drink milk out of a bottle and water out of a specific brand (and size) of sports water bottle. In each case, a major tantrum ensued if they did not have their way. Their inflexibility was beyond what you would see in a typical child.

Some of the inflexibility stems from needing things to be the same. **Children on the autism spectrum become anxious when things change**. For some children it is partly because they have difficulty understanding what will come next and not knowing when the unexpected will end. Therefore predictability is powerful in helping children to cope with change. Other children want things their way all the time. This is in part because children on the autism spectrum tend to be self-focused; their world revolves around their needs to a much greater extent than a typical child. The result is that they experience distress when things don't go their way. That should not mean they are allowed to rule your world. Parents with typical children have rules and boundaries, so should you. It does mean however that you will have to implement the rules in a different way.

In the following sections we revisit two strategies that you have encountered before, gradual desensitization as a strategy for increasing tolerance to change, and the power of predictability.

STRATEGIES FOR CHANGE (FLEXIBILITY)

Gradual Desensitization

Reflect for a moment on how you feel, indeed how we all feel, when confronting something unpleasant, perhaps an activity that makes us anxious or we would rather avoid. The way I think about inflexibility and how to change it is to imagine that we have to massage a knot of resistance, with the goal of easing it out little by little. How do we translate that to changing inflexible behavior in children with autism? Slowly desensitize the child to a different experience by pushing him or her to gradually adapt. We apply the same method as we used in targeting sensory avoidance. If you give in to your child's inflexibility it will not improve. In fact it usually gets worse. Instead if you push your child over time he will adapt. Preschoolers have an incredible ability to change. Don't be put off by the intensity of your child's tantrum. It is not an indicator that making change will be difficult. Use the same strategies that I outlined above. Slowly insist that your child tolerate change for brief periods of time, and slowly increase your expectations.

Make it Predictable

In addition to slowly desensitizing your child to a situation where he exhibits inflexibility, I am going to return to the role of predictability, a topic we discussed earlier. Remember that most **children on the autism spectrum respond better if they have time to prepare for an upcoming activity or change**. As a parent this means that before you expose your child to a change that you know may upset him, provide a warning about what will be different. Keep it very simple. For example, the child who insists on going home the same route each day: you could show him a photo of himself getting in the car (part of his usual routine); then a photo of the grocery store (the new element, that will disrupt his usual route); then a photo of home. Arrange the photos so that he can see all three in order. In the clinic we velcro the photos on a strip of cardboard. You can pair simple language with the photos as you show him "Get ready, first car, then store, then home." Particularly when you know your child may become anxious, it is helpful to show him pictures of the sequence of events. Even if your child understands your language, he may not be able to fully process it if he is anxious. By pairing your language with a picture you are giving him another way to access your communication, and he can hold onto the picture to help him cope with the situation.

Avoid the mistake of thinking that you will tackle your child's inflexibility later on. When we provide support and challenge children to tolerate a situation where things do not go their way they often adapt faster than expected. Being able to accept change and adapt to circumstance is critical for so much in life. Lay the foundation now.

KEY POINTS

- Self-stimulatory behaviors vary widely, they occur in different sensory modes (seeing, touching, hearing, smelling and tasting).

- Abnormal responses to sensory stimuli can interfere with learning.

- To decide if your child's behavior is abnormal or not ask yourself:

    How often is it occurring?

    How long does it last?

    How intense is it?

    How resistant is your child when you prevent the behavior?

- Encourage and teach appropriate ways to get sensory input.

    For sensory seeking: provide alternative means that serve the same sensory function as the inappropriate behavior and redirect inappropriate behaviors.

    For sensory avoidance: gradually desensitize by slowly exposing your child to the unpleasant sensory experience, e.g. vacuum cleaner, wet paint. Work on one goal at a time.

- Increase flexibility earlier rather than later.

- Children on the autism spectrum respond better if they have time to prepare for an upcoming activity or change.

PERSONAL NOTES

9 TREATMENT CHOICES

In this final chapter I want to introduce you to the larger world of treatments for children on the autism spectrum. One could write several books just on treatment options to cover them comprehensively. Rather, this book provides you with specific hands-on strategies that non-professionals can implement immediately. It educates you to intervene in the short term and effectively harness critical time early on in your child's life. It empowers you to begin changing the course of your child's development. However, you also need to find good and appropriate professional therapy for your child which is what this chapter covers.

Most parents would welcome a pharmaceutical cure for their child, or a therapy that would alleviate all of the symptoms. It would be wonderful if it were that simple. Unfortunately, there is no dietary, surgical or drug cure for autism. Instead **therapy and intervention needs to be individualized for each child according to his or her own unique needs and personality.** What works for one child may not work for another. You will find there are many different intervention approaches and opinions about what is effective. The intervention landscape for children on the autism spectrum is not straightforward. This means that you need to become informed about different intervention approaches before making a decision as to what is right for your child.

A broad overview of the different approaches to early intervention will give you perspective and a sense of how to zone in on specific treatments. First I will discuss biomedical interventions, both conventional and unconventional. Then I will provide a framework to help you make sense of the various therapies, interventions and educational approaches. The last three terms (therapy, intervention, educational approach) do not have separate meaning and are often used interchangeably.

This overview will provide you with a framework and a sense of how next to proceed as you read other books and information online, talk with other parents and professionals, and visit clinical and educational settings that have experience with children on the autism spectrum.

UNCONVENTIONAL BIOMEDICAL INTERVENTIONS

One of the first directions that parents are often drawn to is unconventional biomedical interventions. These are practices and products that are not considered part of standard medical care or procedures. They include specific diets like the gluten free casein free (GFCF) diet, dietary supplements such as vitamin B6 and magnesium, dimethylglycine (DMG), anti-fungal medications (e.g. nystatin), and elimination procedures including chelation and heavy metal detoxification. These are some of the 'quick fix' interventions that you will encounter and they are highly unlikely to improve your child's behavior and learning.

The appeal of these 'instant cures' is that they are also easy to sell, especially online, yet there is little evidence that they are effective for children on the autism spectrum. Unfortunately many of these interventions appeal to parents as one can intervene directly and immediately. For parents this is very compelling as it is a food/drug/chemical solution that is, if not easy, at least possible for you to implement. I know there will be a percentage of parents that will want to try them no matter what I say. In the clinic our philosophy is to always support parents as long as there is no potential harm to the child. I know that if I was in your place, I would want to try everything in the hope that something will work. I would probably even want to try treatments that have a very low probability of working. It is understandable why you may be drawn to them.

That said, you should think about several things:

- Most of the alternative treatments have little or no research to support that they actually work. Much of the evidence that is presented is anecdotal (an account of how something worked for a particular child). Remember that autism is a spectrum and the children are surprisingly different in many ways. Be very careful in assuming that anything with anecdotal evidence will help your child. The likelihood is very small.

- Some of the treatments are actually harmful. Be diligent in your research before you try anything.

- Supplements can have negative side effects that can affect your child's behavior and mood.

- Unconventional biomedical treatments are a huge business. Many of the numerous products and services (e.g. laboratory testing) are highly questionable and many are very costly. **Consider carefully how best to use your resources. Focus your finances, time, and psychological resources on treatments that have been shown to have the largest positive impact**. Parents often realize after trying many unconventional quick-fix remedies that the cumulative time and financial cost would have been better spent on longer-term behavioral therapies that are known to work for typical and atypical children.

- Some of the alternative treatments can add further stress to you and your family. The GFCF diet for example, can be an enormous burden on parents who now have to learn how to prepare food without dairy and gluten (often for a child who is already a picky eater). This comes on top of the immense stress that you and your family are already under. You may be thinking that this is irrelevant, that you are willing to do whatever it takes. If that is the case I ask that you go into it having weighed your options well.

CONVENTIONAL PHARMACOLOGICAL TREATMENTS

Most parents of very young children balk at even the slightest idea of giving medication to their child. I completely understand where you are coming from, and in the clinic we seldom bring this up to parents with very young children. However, I do want to mention conventional medications here because they **can be an important part of a good treatment plan** for **some** young children. In other words conventional medication, if necessary, should be used in conjunction with educational and behavioral therapies.

However, there is no single medication or combination of medications that specifically treat autism. Rather, specific symptoms can be successfully treated by a psychiatrist, neurologist or developmental pediatrician with different medications. For example there are medications that alleviate hyperactivity and poor attention, medications that regulate mood, and medications that can increase flexibility. Note that children's responses to medication are different and never assume that what works for one child will necessarily be effective for another. A good physician will always work with parents and other clinicians, therapists, teachers, etc. in finding out what medication and dose works best for your child.

EDUCATIONAL INTERVENTIONS

Comprehensive Treatments

This section provides an overview of educational and behavioral treatments. First there are approaches that are considered comprehensive in that they are intended to intervene in most, if not all, areas of a child's development. These are the main interventions that are often talked about and parents usually hear about applied behavior analysis (ABA) and relationship-based therapy (DIR). The latter is also referred to as Floortime. These are the most well-known of the comprehensive treatments. However instead of just listing the comprehensive treatments, I am going to group them for you in a way that makes them easier to think about. As you hear or read up on various interventions you will then have a better understanding of where they fit philosophically. Very broadly we can think about them in three categories.

The Developmental Approach

The Developmental Approach is child-directed with a focus on establishing an interpersonal relationship with the child. Simply put, the therapist follows the child's interest as a platform for teaching in a naturalistic way. Proponents of this approach argue that learning should occur as naturally as possible. Perhaps the most well known of the developmental therapeutic approaches is DIR (Developmental, Individual-Difference, Relationship-Based Model), also called Floortime, which was developed by Dr. Stanley Greenspan and Serena Wieder. Critics argue that children on the autism spectrum are not learning from the natural environment the way they should, therefore they need a different approach to learn. There is limited research to support the DIR approach.

The Behavioral Approach

The Behavioral Approach uses an individualized curriculum with larger skills broken down into smaller parts. Here the adult drives the interaction and structure. A hierarchy of prompts is used to develop skills from when they are first targeted until the child can independently execute them. To do this, skills are repeatedly practiced. Behavioral methods feel much less natural than child directed teaching as they are highly structured and use strategies that are different from what we use with typical children. Discrete Trial Training (DTT), developed by Dr. Ivar Lovaas, is the most well-known of the behavioral therapies.

Proponents argue that this type of structure is necessary to boost a child's learning and the structure can be gradually decreased towards more natural learning. Critics argue that the approach results in children who interact in an unnatural (or robotic) manner. The behavioral approach, however, is the one that is most supported by research.[1]

Treatments with Behavioral Elements

These interventions have developed out of the behavioral approach. There are several different approaches that fall in this category. They are very different in their philosophies but all come from the same premise that children with autism need an approach that is different than what typical children need. TEEACH (Treatment and Education of Autistic and Related Communication Handicapped Children) was developed by Dr. Eric Schopler at the University of North Carolina. It focuses on strategic use of the environment to maximize independence in children. It is a well-known approach but there is limited research to support its effectiveness. Pivotal Response Training (PRT), developed by Drs. Lynn and Robert Koegel at the University of California Santa Barbara, is also widely used and has a limited number of published studies. It uses teaching in the natural environment to focus on areas that are considered pivotal (e.g. motivation) to change development in children with autism.

Targeted Treatments

In addition to the comprehensive intervention approaches discussed above there are targeted treatments. They do not intervene on the child as a whole or aim to treat all areas of a child's development. Rather they target very specific areas of development. For example the Picture Exchange Communication System (PECS)[2] is a visual communication system; children who cannot yet express themselves verbally can communicate nonverbally using pictures. Other targeted treatments focus on aspects of behavior, aspects of social skills, communication, and academics.

WHAT IS RIGHT FOR MY CHILD?

The problem for parents is that there are few clear answers on what they should do for their child. Professionals disagree on the benefits and limitations of the different intervention approaches, how much intervention a child needs, and how children on the autism spectrum learn. This makes it particularly difficult for parents to make informed decisions.

What We Do Know: The Essentials

Based on my 20+ years of experience working with children on the autism spectrum and on the guidelines published by the National Research Council[1], here is a summary of what we do know:

1. Intervention should begin as **early** as possible.

2. Intervention should be **intensive**. Research still cannot definitively say how many hours a child should receive. An accepted number is around 25 hours total therapy per week. However you should not think of intensity simply as the number of hours; rather think about your child receiving large numbers of functional, developmentally relevant, and highly interesting opportunities to respond actively. This includes family involvement.[1]

3. There is not enough research to suggest that one comprehensive approach is better than another. Be wary of anyone who insists you use only their approach to the exclusion of anything else. Rather it is more important not to rely on one main treatment philosophy (e.g., behavioral or developmental) to address multiple areas of development.

Different approaches in combination are effective, especially when targeting multiple areas of development. You will not hear many clinicians say this, because many still ascribe to the one treatment approach that they learned. This is changing as we become more knowledgeable about children on the autism spectrum.

4. Targeted treatments can significantly add to a comprehensive approach as they are designed to make critical change in a specific area of need. You can use them very effectively in conjunction with other (comprehensive or targeted) interventions. For example the Picture Exchange Communication System (chapter 9), can be used as an effective complement to a comprehensive approach.

5. Children on the autism spectrum learn in **structured developmentally appropriate activities**. Many parents struggle with what is "developmentally appropriate". This is particularly true for first time parents and although I cover this throughout the book, parents may want to refer to a book on typical child development (see resources section). As an additional guide, always ask yourself two questions: When do most typical children learn a particular skill? What other skills did they already learn? This will help you stay within typical developmental milestones and also think about which skills need to be taught before other skills.

6. Intervention should focus on the areas that most affect children on the autism spectrum (communication, social development, appropriate responding to the environment) as covered in detail in this book.

7. There should be a strategic plan with goals that are individualized for your child. You should have a system in place to monitor your child's progress and make changes as you need. For example, your child's goals should be kept in a binder with a clear plan that describes how each goal will be taught, how and when your child's progress will be evaluated and criteria that specify when a goal should be changed. On

any day you should be able to access the binder and easily see what progress your child is making. Of course you should see the same progress in your everyday observations of your child as well. Bi-monthly meetings where you and all therapists are present is another effective way for the team to evaluate intervention effectiveness for each goal and decide where changes are needed.

8. Your child's progress should be assessed regularly in such a way that you can **objectively measure change**. For example, in one week your child progressed from needing maximum prompting to wave bye-bye, to waving bye-bye independently with several family members. You should not be relying on anecdotal, vague updates as a measurement of progress.

9. If your child is not progressing in a goal after a reasonable period of time, something should change. Maybe the goal was too difficult from the outset; maybe the teaching approach should change. Of course what is considered reasonable will depend on what you are trying to achieve. In general, I am uncomfortable if a child does not make progress towards a specific goal in 2 weeks with targeted intervention on that goal for 10 to 15 minutes per day five days a week.

10. The intervention should ensure that your child can use his or her new skills in different contexts (e.g. with different people and in different places). We call this **generalization** and it is covered in chapters 4 and 7.

Use the above 10 points to help you steer a course in your decision making. Use them as a framework to make informed and reasonable decisions.

KEY POINTS

- Unconventional biomedical interventions can have side effects and some are harmful. They also detract from time and resources when behavioral treatments are known to work.

- Pharmacological medications used in conjunction with behavioral treatments can be very effective for some children. Find a physician (psychiatrist, neurologist or developmental pediatrician) who has experience with young children on the autism spectrum.

- A combination of different educational approaches is powerful in making change. Do not become overly focused or sidetracked in finding the 'best' treatment. The most suitable treatment plan for your child can incorporate multiple approaches.

- Use the 10 points at the end of this chapter to guide you in making informed intervention choices for your child regardless of the philosophy or academic debates.

PERSONAL NOTES

CLOSING THOUGHTS:
PARENTING WITH A DIFFERENCE

I know that being a parent is not easy, let alone being a parent with additional challenges and expectations. You all come to this situation with different parenting styles, cultural backgrounds, living situations and levels of support. It is my role to guide you as best I can. It is up to you to find a balance and use the knowledge to the extent that is manageable for you.

There is no doubt that in many ways your parenting will need to be different than parenting a typically developing child. Your child needs more **predictability** and a consistent schedule; strive to plan ahead and be organized. Your child will thrive with **repetition**. Children on the autism spectrum need more practice than other children to learn new concepts and to apply their knowledge in different environments. Recognize that your parenting must suddenly include a great deal more teaching. Think of your role for the next few years not just as a parent, but as a specialist-parent. The strategies in this book are meant to be used within everyday activities. Put your mind and energy to becoming good at implementing the strategies during routines such as meals, bath time, changing a diaper, and when you are out for a walk. Be creative in finding opportunities to practice new skills with your child throughout each day.

If you have family and friends that can help you, use the opportunity to take a break. As much as you will want to do everything you can to help your child, it is vital that you also take time out for yourself. Members of a family are meant to support each other, share life experiences and help each other navigate life's journey. If you pull together, you will not only draw strength from one another but also share in the exciting changes your child will make as you all work together to make it happen. You will be better able to understand and support each other and provide relief to each other. There are other good reasons to involve family. Too often I have seen one spouse become almost estranged from their child, not by choice, but because he or she no longer feels they know how to interact with their son or daughter. This is because your teaching and your child's learning will be constantly evolving; including family hands-on will ensure that they feel comfortable interacting with your child, that they can play an important role in helping to solidify and generalize concepts and that they can help you maintain perspective.

Consistency is not to be underestimated. Children on the autism spectrum learn concepts faster when they are taught the same way repeatedly. This means that every family member (spouse, grandparents, extended family, even a babysitter) should be practicing a new concept in the same way. This includes having the same expectations, using the same language, the same prompts and responses. To some of you it may sound daunting but the truth is that the more consistent you can all be in your interactions, the faster your child will learn and change. Good communication will be vital. Give them chapters of the book to read so that they understand what you are trying to achieve and how to get there. Update each other daily, show how you work on a particular skill. Above all, strive to be positive and supportive of each other.

You can play an enormous role in changing your child's development. Yes, it will require new learning and challenges on your part. It will require ongoing communication, patience, focus and creativity, but it will also bring enormous satisfaction and results. You will be empowered to teach your child, you will celebrate so many more small things on a daily basis than many other parents, and most importantly you will revel in your child's achievements.

Thank-you for reading this book. I hope it brings you many hours of practical and exciting instruction, and joyful times with your child. The book is intended to empower parents; you will be rewarded by returning to the parent friendly teaching strategies over and over again. Just as it takes time to see the fruits of one's labor with typically developing children, the same holds true for children on the autism spectrum. May you and your family celebrate every moment of progress.

With Love and Support

Tanya Paparella

APPENDIX

MODIFIED CHECKLIST FOR AUTISM IN TODDLERS (M-CHAT)

Please fill out the following about how your child usually is. Please try to answer every question. If the behavior is rare (e.g., you've seen it once or twice), please answer as if the child does not do it.

1. Does your child enjoy being swung, bounced on your knee, etc.?   Yes No

2. Does your child take an interest in other children?
Yes No

3. Does your child like climbing on things, such as up stairs?
Yes No

4. Does your child enjoy playing peek-a-boo/hide-and-seek?
Yes No

5. Does your child ever pretend, for example, to talk on the phone or take care of a doll or pretend other things?
Yes No

6. Does your child ever use his/her index finger to point, to ask for something?   Yes No

7. Does your child ever use his/her index finger to point, to indicate interest in something?   Yes No

8. Can your child play properly with small toys (e.g. cars or blocks) without just mouthing, fiddling, or dropping them?
Yes No

9. Does your child ever bring objects over to you (parent) to show you something?   Yes No

10. Does your child look you in the eye for more than a second or two?   Yes No

11. Does your child ever seem oversensitive to noise? (e.g., plugging ears)   Yes   No

12. Does your child smile in response to your face or your smile? Yes   No

13. Does your child imitate you? (e.g., you make a face-will your child imitate it?)   Yes   No

14. Does your child respond to his/her name when you call? Yes   No

15. If you point at a toy across the room, does your child look at it?   Yes   No

16. Does your child walk?   Yes   No

17. Does your child look at things you are looking at?   Yes   No

18. Does your child make unusual finger movements near his/her face?   Yes   No

19. Does your child try to attract your attention to his/her own activity?   Yes   No

20. Have you ever wondered if your child is deaf?   Yes   No

21. Does your child understand what people say?   Yes   No

22. Does your child sometimes stare at nothing or wander with no purpose?   Yes   No

23. Does your child look at your face to check your reaction when faced with something unfamiliar?   Yes   No

SCORING THE M-CHAT

A child fails the checklist when 2 or more critical items are failed OR when any three items are failed.

Yes/no answers convert to pass/fail responses.

Below are listed the failed responses for each item on the M-CHAT. Bold capitalized items are CRITICAL items.

Not all children who fail the checklist will meet criteria for a diagnosis on the autism spectrum.

However, children who fail the checklist should be evaluated in more depth by the physician or referred for a developmental evaluation with a specialist.

1. No	6. No	11. Yes	16. No	21. No
2. NO	**7. NO**	12. No	17. No	22. Yes
3. No	8. No	**13. NO**	18. Yes	23. No
4. No	**9. NO**	**14. NO**	19. No	
5. No	10. No	**15. NO**	20. Yes	

Children who fail more than 3 items total or 2 critical items should be referred for diagnostic evaluation by a specialist trained to evaluate ASD in very young children. However it does not necessarily mean that your child has autism.

In this book the M-CHAT is referred to in Chapter 2.

GLOSSARY

Applied Behavior Analysis (ABA): This is an umbrella term used to describe the study of behavior and change in behavior. It is used to assess and treat behavior and learning using a variety of methods such as analyzing behavior and learning by breaking it down into component parts, teaching sub skills systematically to achieve a larger goal, ensuring generalization, adult directed teaching, repeated practice, and reinforcement. Discrete Trial Training is one teaching approach that falls under the ABA philosophy. You will find the term "Applied Behavior Analysis" in chapter 9.

Auditory Behaviors: This term refers to behaviors that provide a child with sensory input in the auditory modality. In children on the autism spectrum they usually refer to inappropriate behaviors that are characterized by sound. The term is used in chapter 8.

Auditory Processing: Some children have difficulty processing specific language when there are background sounds. They cannot filter out the non-relevant sounds and attend to the relevant language. You will find the term in chapter 3.

Autism Spectrum Disorder (ASD): This is a complex neurological disorder that is evident under 3 years of age. It affects a child in the areas of language, social development and behavior. ASD is described in chapter 2.

Behavioral Approach: In Behavioral Intervention the adult drives the interaction and structure. Teaching goals are based on an individualized curriculum with larger skills broken down into smaller parts. A hierarchy of prompts is used to develop skills from when they are first targeted until the child can independently execute them. To do this, skills are repeatedly practiced. Applied Behavior Analysis is the umbrella term used to describe a variety of teaching methods that use a behavioral approach. The best known is Discrete Trial Training. The Behavioral Approach is described in chapter 9.

Contingent Language: Language that corresponds with the child's focus of attention, i.e. language that matches where the child is already looking. Contingent language is described in chapters 3 and 5.

Desensitization: This is also referred to as Systematic Desensitization. It is a type of behavioral therapy used to overcome anxiety of specific stimuli. Desensitization is discussed in chapter 8.

Developmental Approach: This is an umbrella term used to describe a teaching philosophy that is child-directed and focuses on establishing an interpersonal relationship with the child. The best known treatment approach is called Floortime or Relationship Based Therapy (DIR). Developmental Approaches are described in chapter 9.

Discrete Trial Training (DTT): One method of teaching within the larger philosophy of Applied Behavior Analysis. DTT is explained in chapters 4 and 9 and used in chapter 7 to teach imitation.

Dyadic Interactions: This term refers to an interaction that involves two people engaging face-to-face. Dyadic Interactions are described in chapter 5.

Echolalia: Immediate echolalia is the exact repetition of someone else's speech, immediately or soon after the child hears it. The term delayed echolalia describes speech that is repeated verbatim after some time has passed, i.e. from a one minute delay to a delay of a week or more. Echolalia used to be considered non-functional, but is now thought to serve a communicative purpose.

Emotional Contagion: This describes the process that occurs when a one person reacts to another person's emotional expression by showing the same emotion. In other words one person "catches" and shares the other person's emotion. The concept is described in chapter 5.

Errorless Learning: This behavioral technique is used to teach children new concepts where prompting is provided at the same time as the instruction is given to the child. Errors are prevented by providing as much prompting as needed for the child to be successful and receive reward and social praise. The new skill is repeatedly practiced in this manner and prompts are gradually reduced until the child can respond independently. Errorless Learning is described in chapter 4.

Floortime: A developmental child directed teaching approach that focuses on establishing an interpersonal relationship with the child. It is also known as Relationship-Based Therapy (DIR). Floortime is described in chapter 9.

Generalization: The ability to transfer a new concept or skill from where and how it was initially learned to different contexts. Generalization is discussed in chapters 4 and 7.

Itsy Bitsy Spider: A popular nursery rhyme, also known as "Incy Wincy Spider". It is sung with gestures that describe the actions in the song. It is used in chapter 5.

Joint Attention: This is when a child communicates purely to share experiences with others. The reason for the child's communication is social. This is in contrast to requesting where a child communicates to receive help. Joint attention is discussed in chapter 6.

Language Processing: This is an auditory disorder that involves difficulty understanding spoken language. It is not the result of other cognitive, language, or related disorders. The term is mentioned in chapter 3.

M-CHAT: This is an acronym for the Modified Checklist for Autism in Toddlers. It is used for screening toddlers to assess risk for an autism spectrum disorder. See chapter 2 and the appendix.

Oral Input: This term refers to behaviors that provide a child with sensory input in and around the mouth. The term is used in chapter 8.

Olfactory Input: This term refers to behaviors that provide a child with sensory input related to smell. The term is used in chapter 8.

Picture Exchange Communication System (PECS): This is a picture based communication system used as alternative to spoken language. It is mentioned in chapter 9.

Peek-a-Boo: This is a face-to-face game played with babies and young children where the adult hides their face, then uncovers it and either says "peek-a-boo" or "I see you!" The game is described in chapter 5.

Pivotal Response Training (PRT): This is a treatment approach that uses teaching in the natural environment to focus on areas that are considered pivotal (e.g. motivation) to change development in children with autism. It has elements of the behavioral approach. PRT is mentioned in chapter 9.

Point to Request: A gesture where the index finger is extended toward an object and the purpose of the gesture is used to make a request. It is discussed in chapter 4.

Point to Share: This can also be referred to as Point for Joint Attention. It is a gesture where the index finger is extended toward an object to draw attention to it, comment on it or share interest in it. Pointing to share attention is discussed in chapter 6.

Prompting: This is a teaching strategy where either a model or different degrees of verbal or physical help are provided to the child to ensure he or she is successful in achieving the desired skill. Prompting is discussed in chapter 4.

Proprioceptive Input: This term refers to behaviors that provide a child with sensory input to the joints and muscles. The term is used in chapter 8.

Relationship-Based Therapy (DIR): A developmental child directed teaching approach that focuses on establishing an interpersonal relationship with the child. It is also known as Floortime. See chapter 9.

Ringstack: A toy where a child stacks several donut shaped rings on top of each other on a center pole. The rings differ in size; the largest ring is placed on the bottom and the smallest ring completes the stack on top. For a photo and discussion of how the ringstack is used in teaching imitation see chapter 7 (Imitation, Plan for Success).

Shared Looks: This is a nonverbal means of sharing experience, or engaging in joint attention, where a child shifts their gaze between an object or activity and an adult. The purpose of the communication is purely to engage the other person in a shared experience or enjoyment. Shared looks are discussed in chapter 6.

Show: This is a gesture where a child extends their hand towards you and holds up an object for you to see. They do not release the object because their intention is not to give it you. Rather, their intention is to hold up something for you to see so that you can share their interest. See chapter 6.

Sensory Avoiders: Children who avoid sensory experiences rather than seek them out. These children are sensory avoidant; they become distressed when they come into contact with certain sensory experiences. See chapter 8.

Sensory Seekers: Children who have a high need for certain types of sensory stimuli. A child may seek input in one or more sensory modalities, for example tactile, visual, oral, olfactory and proprioceptive. Chapter 8 discusses sensory seeking behaviors.

Spectrum Disorder: Autism is a spectrum disorder. This means that there is large variation or spectrum in symptom presentation.

Stimming: This is an abbreviated and commonly used term for self stimulate. The term appears in chapter 8.

Tactile Behaviors: This term refers to behaviors that provide a child with sensory input related to smell. The term is used in chapter 8.

TEEACH (Treatment and Education of Autistic and Related Communication Handicapped Children): This is a treatment approach that developed from a behavioral teaching philosophy. It focuses on strategic use of the environment to maximize independence in children. See chapter 9.

Unconventional Biomedical Interventions: These are practices and products that are not considered part of standard medical care or procedures. The topic appears in chapter 9.

Visual Cue: This is a means of providing a prompt that the learner receives visually. They are effective for children who have difficulty understanding what they hear verbally. The visual image can be used to help children learn, remember and anticipate what is coming next. Visual cues are discussed in chapter 3.

Xylophone: A tuned musical instrument that looks similar to a keyboard, however a mallet is used to strike the bars. For a photo and discussion of how the xylophone is used in teaching see chapter 7 (Imitation, Plan for Success).

REFERENCES

Chapter 1

1. Centers for Disease Control (CDC), Atlanta, GA, USA. http://www.cdc.gov/ncbddd/autism/data.html

2. Sutera, S., Pandey, J., Esser, E. L., Rosenthal, M. A., Wilson, L. B., Barton, M., Green, J., Hodgson, S., Robins, D. L., Dumont-Mathieu, T. & Fein, D. (2007). Predictors of optimal outcome in toddlers diagnosed with autism spectrum disorders. *Journal of Autism and Developmental Disorders, 37,* 98-107.

3. Dawson, G. (2008). Early behavioral intervention, brain plasticity, and the prevention of autism spectrum disorder. *Development and Psychopathology, 20,* 775-803.

4. Kasari, C., Freeman, S. F., Paparella, T., Wong, C., Kwon, S. & Gulsrud, A. (2005). Early intervention on core deficits in autism. *Clinical Neuropsychiatry, 2,* 380-388.

5. Kasari, C., Freeman, S. F. & Paparella, T. (2006). Joint attention and symbolic play in young children with autism: A randomized controlled intervention study. *Journal of Psychology and Psychiatry, 47,* 611-620.

6. Kasari, C., Paparella, T. & Freeman, S. F. (2008). Language outcome in autism: Randomized comparison of joint attention and play interventions. *Journal of Consulting and Clinical Psychology,76,* 125-137.

7. Weiss, M. J., Fiske, K. & Ferraioli, S. (2009). Treatment of Autism Spectrum Disorders. In J. L. Matson, F. Andrasik & M. L. Matson (Eds.), *Treating Childhood Psychopathology and Developmental Disabilities*, New York, NY: Springer Science and Business Media, LLC.

Chapter 2

1. Diagnostic and Statistical Manual of Mental Disorders Fourth Edition - Text Revision (DSMIV-TR). American Psychiatric Association.

2. Robins, D., Fein, D. Barton, M. & Green, J. (2001). The modified checklist for autism in toddlers: An initial study investigating the early detection of autism and pervasive developmental disorders. *Journal of Autism and Developmental Disorders, 31*, 131-144.

Chapter 3

1. Paparella, T. & Kasari, C. (2004). Joint attention in special needs populations: A review. *Infants and Young Children,17*, 269-280.

Chapter 5

1. Behrmann, M., Cibu, T. & Humphreys, K. (2006). Seeing it differently: Visual processing in autism. *Trends in Cognitive Sciences, 10,* 258-264.

Chapter 6

1. Stone, W. & Yoder, P. (2001). Predicting spoken language level in children with autism spectrum disorders. *Autism: The International Journal of Research and Practice, 5,* 341-361.

2. Charman, T., Taylore, E., Drew, A., Cockerill, H., Brown, J. & Baird, G. (2005). Outcome at 7 years of children diagnosed with autism at age 2: Predictive validity of assessments conducted at 2 and 3 years of age and pattern of symptom change over time. *Journal of Child Psychology and Psychiatry, 46,* 500-513.

3. Kasari, C., Paparella, T. & Freeman, S. F. (2008). Language outcome in autism: Randomized comparison of joint attention and play interventions. *Journal of Consulting and Clinical Psychology, 76, 125-137.*

4. Kasari, C., Freeman, S. F. & Paparella, T. (2006). Joint attention and symbolic play in young children with autism: A randomized controlled intervention study. *Journal of Psychology and Psychiatry, 47,* 611-620.

Chapter 9

1. National Research Council (NRC) (2001). Educating Children with Autism. Washington, DC: National Academy Press.

2. Bondy, A. & Frost, L. (1994). The picture exchange communication system. *Focus on Autistic Behavior, 9,* 1–19.

RESOURCES

Organizations

American Academy of Pediatrics (AAP)
(847) 434-4000 www.aap.org/healthtopics/autism.cfm
Provides information on identifying autism and treatment.

Autism Society of America (ASA)
(301) 657-0881 www.autism-society.org
Has information on many topics including a US online directory
of resources.

Autism Speaks
(212) 332-3580 www.autismspeaks.org
Advocates for individuals with autism and their families. Funds
research investigating the causes and treatments for autism.

Center for Autism Research and Treatment (CART)
Semel Institute, UCLA
(310) 267-2778 http://www.semel.ucla.edu/autism
Offers community education and opportunities to be involved in
research.

Centers for Disease Control and Prevention (CDC)
(800) 232-4636 www.cdc.gov/ncbddd/autism
Provides general information for parents on screening,
diagnosis, symptoms and treatment.

Cure Autism Now
(888) 828-8476 www.canfoundation.org
Provides general information, a resource database and research
initiatives.

Families for the Early Autism Treatment (FEAT)
(916) 303-7405   www.feat.org
Provides parent support and information on education, advocacy
and resources.

MIND Institute
(916) 703-0280   www.ucdmc.ucdavis.edu/mindinstitute/
Research center focused on neurodevelopmental disorders.
Website provides education and resources for families and
opportunities to be involved in research.

**National Dissemination Center for Children with Disabilities
(NICHCY)**
(800) 695-0285   www.nicycy.org/resources.autism.asp
Provides resources in each state.

National Institutes of Health (NIH)
(301) 496-4000   www.nichd.nih.gov/autism/
www.nichd.nih.gov/publications/pubs/autism/facts/index.htm
A medical research agency that is part of the United States
Department of Health and Human Services. NIH funds
international medical research and provides outreach and
education to the public.

National Institute of Mental Health (NIMH)
(866) 615-6464   www.nimh.nih.gov/publicat/autism.cfm
An agency of the United States Department of Health and
Human Services and part of NIH. It is the largest research
organization in the world specializing in mental illness. Provides
education to the public.

Pervasive Developmental Disorder (PDD) Support Network
www.autism-pdd.net
Provides online support for parents.

Zero to Three

(202) 638-1144 www.zerotothree.org

Nonprofit organization that provides guidelines and education on development in typical infants and toddlers.

Useful Books

The Baby Book: Everything you Need to Know about your Child from Birth to Age 2. William Sears, M.D. and Martha Sears, R.N. Publisher: Little Brown, 2003.

Caring for Your Baby and Young Child, 5th Edition: Birth to Age 5. Steven P. Shelov, MD, MS, FAAP. Publisher: Bantam, 2009.

Does My Child Have Autism? A Parent's Guide to Early Detection and Intervention in Autism Spectrum Disorders. Wendy L. Stone, Ph.D. and Theresa Foy DiGeronimo, M.Ed. Publisher: Jossey-Bass, 1st Edition, 2006.

Could it be Autism? A Parent's Guide to the First Signs and Next Steps. Nancy D. Wiseman. Publisher: Broadway, 1st Edition, 2006.

The First Year®: Autism Spectrum Disorders: An Essential Guide for the Newly Diagnosed Child. Nancy D. Wiseman. Publisher: Da Capo Press, 2009.

Overcoming Autism: Finding the Answers, Strategies, and Hope that Can Transform a Child's Life. Lynn Kern Koegel, Ph.D. and Claire LaZebnik. Publisher: Penguin Group, 2004.

Play and Engagement in Early Autism: The Early Start Denver Model. Sally Rogers, Ph.D. and Geraldine Dawson, Ph.D. Publisher: Guilford Publishing, 2009.

More than Words: Helping Parents Promote Communication and Social Skills in Children with Autism Spectrum Disorder. Fern Sussman. Publisher: Hanen Center, 2009.

Educating Children with Autism. Catherine Lord and J. McGee, eds. Publisher: National Academy Press, 2001.

Right From the Start: Behavioral Intervention for Young Children with Autism. Sandra L. Harris, Ph.D. and Mary Jane Weiss, Ph.D., BCBA. Publisher: Woodbine House, 2nd Edition, 2007.

CPSIA information can be obtained at www.ICGtesting.com
Printed in the USA
LVOW05s2339061113

360259LV00005B/1127/P